Chancery | Government House | Yarralumla 1994

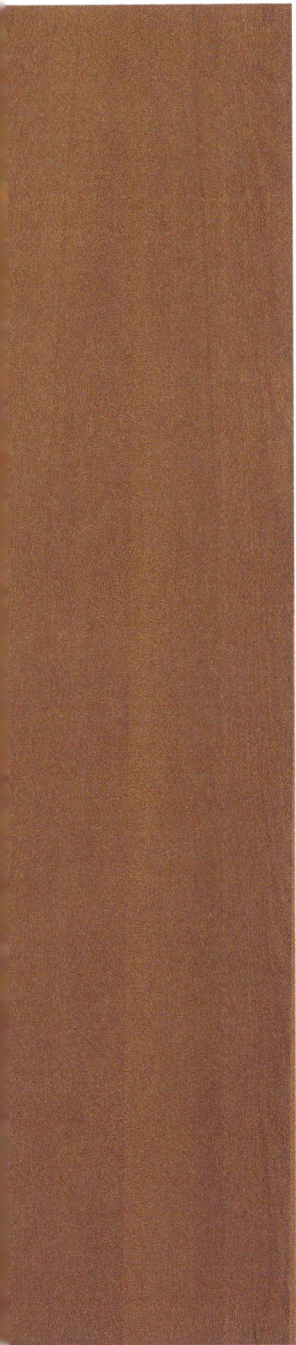

First Published in 2021 by Echo Books

Echo Books is an imprint of Superscript Publishing Pty Ltd, ABN 76 644 812 395

Registered Office: Suite 401, 140 Bourke St, Melbourne, VIC, 3000

www.echobooks.com.au

Author: Judd, Nathan G

Title: A Canberra Architect: Roger Pegrum

ISBN: 978-0-6488545-1-7 (Hardcover)

A catalogue record for this book is available from the National Library of Australia

Book design by Peter Gamble, Canberra. Cover illustration by Luke Bicevskis
Set in Helvetica Light, 9/11.

(((echo)))
BOOKS

A CANBERRA
ARCHITECT
ROGER PEGRUM

Nathan G Judd

07   **08**

Foreword

Roger Pegrum's contribution to the development of Canberra and his national commitment to architecture and planning has elevated the profile of the city as a capital of quality and national value. He is truly the Bush Capital architect.

Roger's family settled in Canberra in 1948 having migrated from England—he was ten years old. The provisional (now 'Old') Parliament House had been opened only twenty years earlier. The Griffin Plan for the city had barely been sketched into the landscape and Lake Burley Griffin would not be realised for another sixteen years. Roger enjoyed the landscape and the inland bush setting that in many perceptions is quintessentially Australia. He grew up watching and enjoying the buzz of a city in the making and he developed a strong passion for design that has remained with him throughout his life.

Roger left Canberra to study architecture at the University of Sydney having taken up a cadetship with the Commonwealth Department of Works. After graduating he returned to the city and began to make his mark in public works. He met fascinating and knowledgeable people along the way and thoroughly enjoyed the breadth of work that this opportunity afforded. So began a long love affair with public architecture that would culminate in his appointment in 1986 as the Commonwealth Director of Architecture—the last as fate would have it and the first to publish many of its achievements.

In the years between he travelled overseas to see and learn and live life to the fullest. Together with his twin brother Anthony, he established a highly successful architectural practice in Canberra which included houses that remain a hallmark of quality and desire in the Canberra residential environment.

Roger left Canberra in 1974 to take up an academic appointment to the University of Sydney in the Faculty of Architecture. He became what was rare in those days—a prolific and widely respected architecture and planning commentator across all media.

He embraced the public as his audience rather than only the profession. He initiated and compiled two volumes of *Details in Australian Architecture*, ground-breaking publications that married practical approaches to building construction with design sensibility. He was more than 'busy'—he influenced architecture in a positive and lively manner.

In 1983 Roger extended his Master of Town and Country Planning thesis and published *The Bush Capital: How Australia chose Canberra as its Federal City*. That work is arguably the first 'story' of Canberra to be widely read and the first to make the 'Bush Capital' a populist descriptor for our National Capital city.

There is little that Roger Pegrum has not done as an architect. He has been deeply engaged with the profession serving on the Australian Institute of Architects ACT Chapter Council, participating on multiple design juries, entering and winning many design competitions, publishing widely, providing opinion as an expert witness and being a member of government tribunals, advisory committees and governance councils and contributing to architectural education.

This book includes some of Roger Pegrum's work as an architect with a special focus on Canberra. It has been compiled by Nathan G Judd, his son-in-law and also a Canberra architect, with contributions from his family to mark and celebrate his 80th birthday.

Roger is a fine Australian architect but he is also a man of great passion with strong personal values and integrity. He lives his life fully, engages with 'the many' and has won the respect and love of all of his family. I am proud to be his wife.

Annabelle Pegrum

Reid House

A Life Engaged

Elisabeth Judd

In a career spanning more than 50 years, Roger Pegrum has established a legacy as one of Canberra's founding architects and a reputation as an articulate commentator on design, planning and city-making. Through his work in private practice, as an academic and in government service he has become an enduring example of a professional committed to excellence in his field.

Arriving in Canberra in 1948 as a young boy he was impressed by the potential of the city and the vision of those who aspired to its future. Who could not be in awe at the audacity of creating a new national capital on a sheep station! Almost by osmosis, he would experience the emergence of one of the great planned cities of the world—an example unparalleled in Australia of a city that has come of age in the span of a generation. Pegrum has embraced this history, drawing on his 'home town' experience to enrich the debate on the pitfalls and potential of town planning and contributing to critical strategic decisions that have shaped the urban fabric of Canberra—our Bush Capital.

From 1961-63 and again in 1965-67, Pegrum worked as a graduate architect in the Commonwealth Department of Works. One of only a 'handful' of graduates at that time, Pegrum was given the unique opportunity to work on a number of projects that would prove to have a lasting legacy in the city—not the least of which included the design of the front entrance and portico at Old Parliament House, and internal refurbishments of the Cabinet Room and offices of Gough Whitlam. On secondment to the relatively newly established National Capital Development Commission in 1963, he worked with Sir William Holford on the design of Anzac Parade. Pegrum was tasked with designing the ceremonial street lighting—the resulting 'string of pearls' created a delicate beading of light to line the vista from Parliament House to the War Memorial. As new suburban districts emerged to house the next generation of Canberra families, Pegrum was also responsible for the design of the first primary schools in Woden, including for Hughes, Garran and Mawson. It could be argued that these buildings contributed to the first experiences of public architecture for many young Canberrans.

Pegrum's contribution as a public servant came full circle in the late 1980s. Following 12 years in Sydney he returned to Canberra as Director of Architecture and First Assistant Secretary in the Department of Housing and Construction. 'Frank and fearless' in his advice to government at state and federal levels, he worked with vigour against any approach that would reduce the value of public buildings to the lowest commercial denominator and was a strong advocate of the value of the Department. His book *Australian Government Architects* celebrated the achievements of architectural and engineering staff and included important critical essays by Neville Quarry and Roger Johnson.

In 1968, Pegrum commenced his career in private practice. This has yielded a portfolio of buildings renowned for their quality and recognised professionally by nearly 30 awards, including the Canberra Medallion and the 25 Year Award for Enduring Architecture. During the 1970s his work defined an emerging era in Canberra residential architecture. His use of natural materials and space and light in houses which responded to Canberra's unique and beautiful bush setting was instrumental in contributing to a new direction for design in the city—one influenced more by our natural Australian heritage and less by the colonial past. His private commissions have included an enviable range of buildings in Canberra over the last five decades including private residences, multi-residential developments, government and university buildings, schools, health centres, heritage refurbishments and a soccer stadium. He has been awarded prizes in a number of urban design and architectural competitions including

for City Hill in Canberra, the Sydney Showgrounds, the Education Building at the University of Sydney and the Chancery at Government House in Yarralumla. His work is always meticulous, elegant and robust and never loses sight of the client brief.

Throughout his career, Pegrum has sought to encourage engagement by the community and professionals in discussions on architecture, planning and good design. From 1974 to 1986 he worked as a senior lecturer and then associate professor in the Department of Architecture at Sydney University. In this role he taught design as well as construction courses to a new generation of architects, some of whom have gone on to establish themselves as leading Australian architects. His *Details in Australian Architecture* publications were considered seminal texts by students for decades. As a lecturer he earned a reputation as an instructive and insightful mentor, encouraging critical analysis and inspiring his students to consider the basis of great architecture and to aspire to achieve it.

Pegrum has been a prolific writer, authoring a number of books as well as contributing to other authors' works, publishing more than 70 articles to date including for the *Australian*, *The Canberra Times* and *Architecture Australia*, and crafting strategic policy documents. His writing has helped to bring architecture to the wider Canberra community, provoking discourse on topical issues of urban design, planning regulation and the built environment and celebrating good design. In 1973 he was awarded the RAIA HAL Scholarship to research housing for the elderly. The resulting publication *The Architecture of Old Age: a study of the relationship of older people with the built environment* remains current with debate continuing on this critical issue. And his 1977 article 'The Job for a Genius' critiqued the then proposed procurement for the new Parliament House, successfully arguing for a wider design competition which ultimately resulted in the acclaimed building now occupying Capital Hill. More recently he prepared 'Garden City Values and Principles' for the ACT Government. And in 2016 his article in *Architecture Australia* describing the winning competition entry for the Bowen Place Crossing skilfully wove together a tale of Canberra's past with discussion on the need for high quality urban infrastructure to meet the challenges of our future urban landscape.

True to form, Pegrum's insatiable curiosity and lust for life have led him to also engage in a range of community pursuits, including as a member of the Magna Carta Committee, the Governing Council of Old Parliament House and the ACT Heritage Council. He has been a planning adviser to St John's Church for development of the Constitution Avenue Precinct and has offered various talks on Canberra's landscape and cultural heritage in a range of forums including for Rotary, the University of the Third Age and the Canberra International Music Festival. He has delivered occasional lectures at the University of Canberra and the Canberra Institute of Technology on planning theory and construction technology, and has even managed coaching of a high school hockey team.

His considerable professional experience and knowledge of design, construction and planning has also afforded him a place as a Senior Member of the ACT Civil and Administrative Tribunal. Roger Pegrum's body of work as an architect is enhanced by his significant commitment to his profession. An active member of the Australian Institute of Architects (RAIA) since 1961, Pegrum has served on awards juries for the ACT, NSW and Northern Territory Chapters and the Institute's national awards, and has held various chapter roles including as vice-president and honorary treasurer. Continuing his contribution to architectural construction he was a member of the Architects' Accreditation Council visiting panel for the Universities of NSW, Newcastle, Adelaide and the Universities of Auckland and Victoria at Wellington and has also served as an examiner for the Architects Board of the ACT. In 2004 Pegrum was awarded a RAIA ACT Chapter President's Medal for assisting the community following the devastating Canberra bushfires in January 2003. And in 2009 his work and career were recognised by award of an RAIA Life Fellowship. In its citation the Institute noted that 'few architects in Australia have made such a continuous, diverse and meaningful contribution to the advancement of architecture over such a long period of time'.

Roger Pegrum continues to design, to write, to engage, provoke and motivate. His contribution to the urban fabric of Canberra and to the debate about matters of strategic significance is indisputable. He is an inspiration to the next generation of architects, planners and urban thinkers.

Roger has rendered notable contributions to the advancement of the profession of architecture over many years. This contribution has taken many forms including a distinguished record in practice, architecture education and policy, publication and promotion of architecture, professional service and community contribution. Roger's achievements in design have been recognised in his invitations to be a member of the Institute's National Jury and as a member of a number of Chapter juries. He is also truly one of the founding architects of Canberra.

Few architects in Australia have made such a continuous, diverse and meaningful contribution to the advancement of architecture over such a long period of time.

Citation—RAIA Life Fellowship, 2009

Government House Chancery

The Early Houses

Manor Houses: 1968–74

The Early Houses

Marcus Trimble

Introduction

On returning from England in 1966 Pegrum completed his five year cadetship with the Commonwealth Department of Works. It was during this time that he purchased a block of land in the new suburb of Garran and built his first home for his family. This project served as the impetus to set up an office and within a month of moving into the house Roger Pegrum had opened an office in Civic.

Through a strategically placed advertisement in *The Canberra Times*, the practice was busy with work within three hours of opening its door—the happy confluence of professional enthusiasm and an optimistic city. During the first years of practice, work covered a range of commissions from schools to aged care housing along with a steady stream of residential projects. With these houses, the domestic realm became a venue for exploration and the refinement of Pegrum's architectural craft and intent. It was in the houses that the material quality of building elements was explored and it was here that the act of building places for people became the dominant characteristic of much of Pegrum's ongoing career.

Roger's twin brother Anthony (Tony) joined the practice in mid-1968 and brought with him clients who were older and entwined in the political landscape of the ACT at the time. Tony Pegrum had been a partner at the well established office of John Scollay and Theo Bischoff and the clients that he brought with him included professors at the Australian National University, secretaries of federal government departments and senior officers from the Military College in Duntroon. These clients were a rare breed of bureaucrat and academic—a sector of the community that does not appear to be thriving today—who were willing to engage in architecture with the same level of purpose with which they approached their life and their work. They were experts in their fields and understood the good faith necessary to encourage an environment of innovation and well crafted thoughts. As such the houses that were designed for them by Roger and Tony Pegrum were contemporary and daring.

Landscape

Many of the projects completed by Pegrum in the first ten years were in the so-called new towns of Canberra. The National Capital Development Commission (NCDC) planned for growth within the valleys surrounding Canberra, leaving the hillsides free of buildings. The valleys of Woden and Tuggeranong to the south and the plains of Belconnen to the northwest were rapidly filled in with new housing. Known as the 'Y-Plan', the new land releases were generally on steep, hilly sites surrounded by bushland and this landscape served as the background for much of Pegrum's early work.

The suburb of Campbell east of Anzac Parade shows a marked deviation from the formal structure of the older suburb of Reid to the west. In Reid, the streets are laid out in a manner following the original intent of the Griffin's plan with housing that is similarly formal. Streets and houses in Campbell are more responsive to the topography of the site. Streets follow the contour lines of the hills and the houses tend to sit within heavily landscaped gardens.

It is within landscapes like this that Pegrum built his first houses. They show the economy and invention present in many architect's first works. Primarily houses for young families, they are lean while managing to examine the potential of material choice and spatial investigation. But it is landscape that is the common defining characteristic of these early houses. The low lying hills of Canberra, in which many of these houses sit, afford varied topographic opportunities.

From these elements are drawn building typologies of courtyard houses and terraced houses that remain grounded in their place. As in the Sydney School houses of the same era, these used local materials as an expression of regionalism within the modernist framework—timber fascias, face brick walls and native landscaping.

The courtyard is the dominant organisational device in Pegrum's houses during this period. Perhaps atypically, however, the courtyard is rarely completely internal. Instead, it shares only one edge with an interior space and three perimeter walls shielding the court from the landscape beyond. They are not external rooms that provide secondary circulation or bring light into a deep floor plan, rather they are territorial. They reach out and embrace a part of the landscape and claim it as their own, a response to the edgeless nature of Canberra's newer sub-divisions where the property boundaries were not yet entirely defined. The bush capital was just that—bush. As such, private open space had to be captured and contained.

Walker House Campbell, 1963

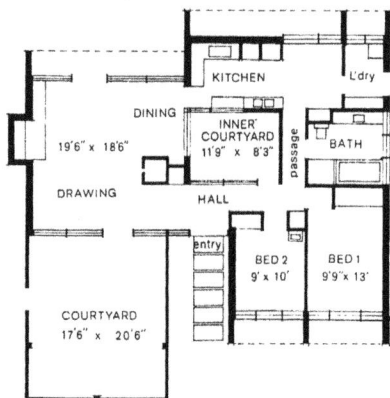

Roger Pegrum

Pegrum House | Garran | 1967

Roger Pegrum built this house for himself and his young family in the Woden Valley suburb of Garran. Here he employed several techniques that disclose this work as that of a young architect with limited means, while seeking to embed the house with the traces of its use as a family home. The property is located at the end of a cul-de-sac following a long line of government owned housing and was one of two blocks that were available for purchase due to their apparently un-buildable topography and the large rocks on the site.

Here Pegrum first employed the strategy that would appear in many later houses—that of the external walled court. Complementing this external court is a smaller internal courtyard around which the rooms of the house are organised.

The house is constructed of recycled sandstock bricks from an old warehouse in Goulburn. Pegrum notes that these walls 'seemed to me to represent the softest imposition on the landscape'. In this, he shared a philosophical ground with Sydney School architects such as Ken Woolley who were at the time examining ways in which to respond to the Australian landscape through rugged material choices.

The house is literally tied to its landscape. The large rocks on the site—a factor in keeping the land price affordable—became advantageous in grounding the house on a solid base, while the planning arrangement placed the wet areas off to the side of the rock to facilitate cheaper construction. Judicious landscaping has resulted in the house now being surrounded by an established native garden. Coupled with the earthy materiality of the masonry walls this has resulted in a house that is deeply embedded in its place.

KITCHEN   L'dry

DINING

INNER COURTYARD 11'9" x 8'3"   BATH

19'6" x 18'6"

passage

DRAWING   HALL

entry

BED 2 9' x 10'   BED 1 9'9" x 13'

COURTYARD 17'6" x 20'6"

Walker House | Campbell | 1963

This house was Roger Pegrum's first private commission and the first of more than 40 private houses he designed in Canberra. The client was a public servant who had been transferred to Canberra from Melbourne. When the original owners returned to Melbourne the property was purchased by Ronald and Pamela Walker who undertook various minor refurbishments with Canberra architects Ric Butt and Clem Cummings and have now lived in the home for almost 50 years.

The suburb of Campbell is on the southern slopes of Mount Ainslie and was the first 'new' residential district laid out in the Canberra valley following the establishment of the National Capital Development Commission in 1957. The site is part of a small parcel of residential land behind the Australian War Memorial.

The floor plan wraps around a sunny courtyard which is sheltered from the prevailing winds and is visible from all major areas of the house. The house is of significance as an intact example of modernist residential design in Canberra with the innovative structural input of the renowned Melbourne engineer Norman Mussen.

The house and gardens are in excellent condition. Rooms are generous in area and volume with attractive outlooks and a pleasing variety of lighting and colour. A range of places for working, eating and relaxing are filled with paintings and objects collected through a long and busy life in Australia and overseas.

Walker House

Vikky Wilkes

Ryan Wight

Wilson House | Aranda | 1972

The Wilson House was awarded the CS Daley Medal of the ACT Chapter of the RAIA for residential architecture in 1974 and in 2005 also received the Institutes 25-Year Award for Enduring Architecture.

This is another house in which the courtyard plays a significant role. A north-facing courtyard is captured as a heavily landscaped garden complete with ponds and a bridge, contained on two sides by the house. The house is planned along a zigzag; the two primary living spaces making up the two legs of the L which encloses the courtyard. A wing containing the bedrooms branches back towards the bush behind. Sharply raking skillion roofs nimbly navigate this bending plan form while providing the living spaces with lofty interiors.

The low eaves of the roofs as they meet the edge of the courtyard compress the threshold with the exterior producing a highly focused and direct relationship with the attractive gardens.

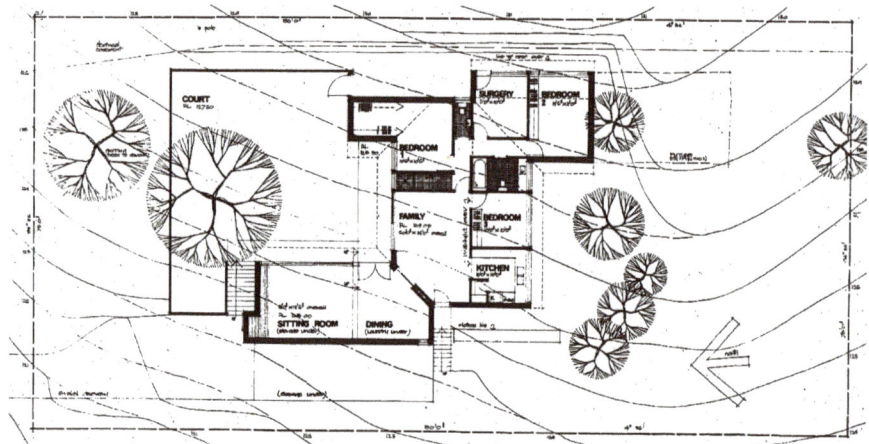

Later additions included a spa and sauna, and the refurbishment of an original bathroom received a further Institute commendation.

20

Byam Wight

Australian Institute of Architects citation 2005

25-Year Award 2005

House at 38 Mirning Crescent, Aranda

by Roger Pegrum

This family home, designed by Roger Pegrum and completed in 1973, was awarded the C.S. Daley Medal in 1974. Built for a local doctor and his family, the building is an accomplished example of the Sydney Regional Style, or Sydney School, in Canberra. It has been entered in the RAIA Register of Significant Twentieth Century Architecture.

The suburb of Aranda was developed in the late 1960s and early 1970s. Its steep topography and natural bush environment provided alternative opportunities for suburban housing in Canberra, which until then had a tradition of highly conventional housing types presenting a respectable face to the street on near level, treeless blocks. With its natural landscape and significant crossfall 38 Mirning Crescent is typical of many Sydney School sites.

The plan is roughly a Z shape. The kitchen, family room and main bedroom run across the site, facing the street. A combined living and dining room extends forward along the western side of the site and further

bedrooms and service rooms extend to the rear along the eastern side. The house is approached via a large courtyard space, screened from the street by a brick wall set back from the front boundary with pleasant native landscaping. The building presents a blank, almost fortress-like wall to the street, flouting the convention of a presentation façade. The exterior form is a bold composition of opposing skillion roof and wall planes which is crisp and sculptural. There is a sense of opposing U shaped forms separated by the clerestory line, which internally defines the major and minor spaces, and externally the focus to the front and rear courtyards.

The building is well built using a limited palette of traditional materials in an innovative and well detailed manner and remains in excellent condition. Cavity brick walls are left as unpainted commons externally and bagged and painted internally. The roof is Roman pattern tiles. Windows and doors are black painted timber and interior trim is clear finished Ash. The interiors although now furnished in a different fashion from the originally completed house retain the same sense of space, light and airiness providing an enduring backdrop to changing personal tastes.

Alterations and additions completed in 1988 were also designed by Roger Pegrum. These involved a small extension of the kitchen, the addition of a spa room to the rear, the conversion of the original dressing room into a sitting alcove off the main bedroom and the construction of a new dressing room along the eastern side. The kitchen addition echoes the original projecting dressing room (now sitting alcove) and has the same gesture of wrapping the house around the rear outdoor space. The resulting southern courtyard gives the house a dual focus.

These changes embrace the original, highly innovative design philosophy, and add to it. This together with the care of its occupants, and the maturing landscape affords the building a sense of completion.

Conan-Davies House | Aranda | 1968

Described as 'fortress like' by the press at the time, the Conan-Davies house is characterised by solid perimeter walls with slab-like timber clad roofs that step down the sloping site.

This house, like many of Pegrum's houses during this period, is concerned with an examination of the interior, with glazing generally facing into walled courts rather than onto the street, and a focus on the interior activity of its occupants. An engagement with the street, and the manner in which it sits within the landscape was therefore articulated through the volumetric massing of solid elements and discrete entry openings rather than the transparency of large openings.

At the Conan-Davies house, this internalisation is perhaps at its most pronounced. The house is simply arranged; bedrooms and service spaces are off a gallery space with the living and study on a split level half a floor below. The living space opens out to the north onto the walled courtyard with high masonry walls and a single opening. This opening is a doorway however, not a window, suggesting that this aperture is for movement and access, not outlook.

While it is clear that the living room is directly opening out onto the courtyard,

a centrally located fireplace is equally assertive, suggesting the occupants turn their backs to the courtyard, and refocus their attention to the interior.

Pegrum states that this focus on inner character was a response to the landscape at the time. In the sub-divisions of the new towns of Canberra the outlook was not always established thus the houses needed to create their own topography through devices such as split levels and courtyards. The house responds to the sub-urbanism of its context with skillful articulation. Where at the time there were few built precedents, the house responds to its corner position with confident articulation. The brick volume pushes out to the North and slips beneath the overhang of the roof which extends out

to the West, creating a corner that is both eroded yet solid enough to hold the geometry.

The volumetric directness of the house is reinforced by the materials and language of construction. Solid masonry walls—made from bricks salvaged from the demolition of the Goulburn Wool Exchange—wrap around the perimeter of the house. Windows are formed not as openings but by the walls stopping short of the roof, an effect used at the entry where the front door becomes a pulling apart of walls between two L shapes. The roofs are long horizontal planes clad in timber, an established motif that here is expanded upon by folding the plane down at the interface between the living room and the courtyard.

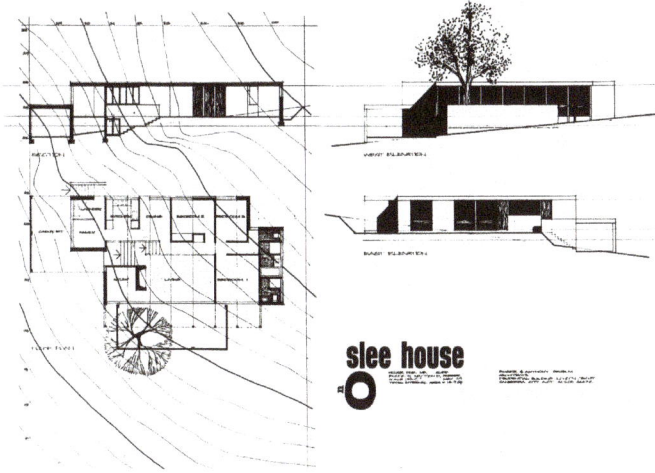

slee house

Slee/Harris House | Farrer | 1969

This house was designed for Mike and Judy Slee on a steep site in Farrer with uninterrupted views of the Woden Valley and the Brindabellas. It has a deceptively simple open plan on two levels with a hallway as a spine. Living spaces are delineated by a low wall and a large brick hearth behind which sits the study. The house was later bought by Rob and Cathie Harris for whom Pegrum refurbished the kitchen and added a family room. The house is otherwise largely unaltered.

Byam Wight

Cumpston House | Aranda | 1970

A large house on three levels for John and Helen Cumpston on the west edge of Black Mountain. The house steps gently down the site and defers to the remnant bush landscape. John was a scholar of Douglas Mawson and the Antarctic and a double height library was included at the top level. Helen was the president of the native garden society in Canberra for many years.

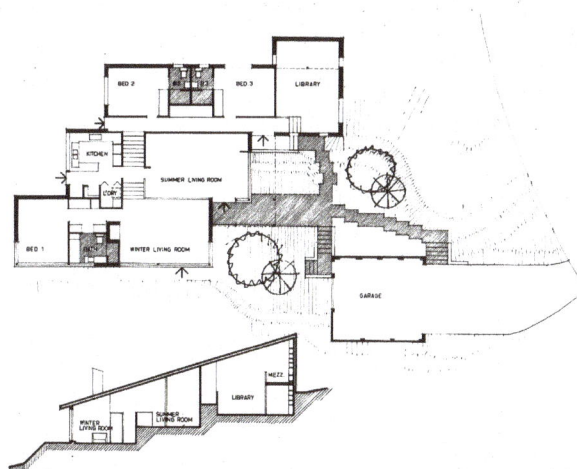

A Government Architect

Nathan G Judd with Roger Pegrum

NJ You were Director of Architecture for the Commonwealth Government from 1986 to 1988—what was your role?

RP This was a magic time, quite unlike anything I had known before. How do you prepare for a position like that? Australia's first Chief Architect was John Smith Murdoch, a Scotsman who had started as a draftsman with Queensland Public Works and transferred to the new Department of Works and Railways soon after Federation. His responsibilities then included design and construction of infrastructure and government buildings, customs houses, defence establishments and so on in all of the States.

NJ So Murdoch essentially evolved into the position?

RP Yes, and the office of the Chief Architect for the Commonwealth has moved about and changed direction for most of its life and is now of course no longer. I share a bit of a bond with Murdoch—he was the first Australian Government Architect and I was the last. When the Parliament moved from Melbourne to Canberra in 1927, the Department of Works and Railways and most of the federal government departments remained in Melbourne. There were name changes to Department of Works and later Housing and Construction. Still working in Melbourne, Murdoch designed many of Canberra's early buildings including the Powerhouse at Kingston and later Parliament House, the Hotel Canberra and the Hotel Kurrajong.

When I joined the Department of Works as a cadet in 1956, the Government Architect was Richard Ure, who worked from the head office in Melbourne. Ure had a deserved design reputation after winning the competition for the Australian-American War

Memorial in Canberra. I came across him on several of his visits to the Canberra office when he reviewed our school designs and commented on our designs for Anzac Parade. Before Ure, the Chief Architect had been John Overall, later appointed

Olympic Swimming Pool Canberra 1955. Department of Works ACT
Ian Slater RAIA Sulman Medal 1955

National Archives of Australia

Australian Pavillion Osaka Japan 1970. Department of Works ACT
James MacCormick, Theo Hirsch, Max Barham, Robin Boyd

as the first Commissioner of the National Capital Development Commission. Subsequent appointments included Peter Hall, who had taken on the challenge to complete the Sydney Opera House after the departure of Joern Utzon. The accomplished Sydney architect Bruce Bowden was my immediate predecessor as Director. A very impressive list of architects really.

Following in the footsteps of these luminaries was a daunting proposition. The head office of what was by then the Department of Housing and Construction had finally moved to Canberra but was on the other side of town and operated quite independently from the ACT regional office. Here I was, straight out of academic life and back where I started. But I saw the Department as well regarded in the profession. I thought it was doing excellent work in many important areas and I was pleased to be back on deck.

NJ So it was a viable government enterprise.

RP I thought so, but maybe it wasn't. It was a demonstrably professional business offering high level services

in architecture, engineering and project management. Perhaps it was too geographically widespread. Operational responsibility was devolved to the regional offices in the States and Territories, but there were no obvious problems of quality or integrity or consistency. At all levels, the Department provided the Commonwealth Government with frank and fearless advice in all aspects of infrastructure and construction. We had experts in airfield design and construction and in building and operating scientific bases in Antarctica. We designed innovative facilities on military bases, we had specialist capacities in the areas of heritage conservation and environmental management and in the last few years we had won several major awards for design.

NJ So was the Department building architecture at the time or was it building buildings?

RP That's a good question. I think they were still trying to build architecture. They were doing this by the simple means of engaging and employing good architects and engineers and landscape architects. If you had a job as an architect in the Department, you

were more likely to be a good one than an ordinary one. That can be demonstrated by the scope of work and by industry recognition and awards. The range of work undertaken by the Department was astonishing. How often would an office get the chance to build a university campus or a family court or an Australian pavilion at an international exposition in Japan? Some incredibly complex things too, buildings to service guided missiles or teach submariners how to avoid the bends. Magnificent hangers in the Northern Territory for beautiful looking FA-18s.

Not everything was that exciting of course, there were always telephone exchanges and army barracks and warehouses. My role in much of this work was obviously limited but I was trying to encourage the best from everybody. It meant I had to spend as much time as possible with younger and older architects in the regional offices listening to their thinking and offering clear advice and direction where needed. Every now and then I made comments that ruffled a few feathers ...

NJ Deterministic?

RP Yes, some of my decisions were not well received, especially about materials and buildability and maintenance, things that can be easily forgotten in the heat of the design moment. My argument was that the Commonwealth was one of the few commissioning bodies that kept the things they built, did not wash its hands of them. We couldn't just walk away as a mean spirited developer might have done. Creativity must recognise function and lifetime costs as well as visual attractiveness. In the short time I was in this position I rightly or wrongly condemned a few new age building materials and banned them from the Departmental palette. It was the same with detailing for construction, we must take care to see that our buildings will stand the test of time. When I was a student and then a very junior architect in the local office of the Department there was a senior architect whose only interest in what I was drawing was whether it could be built easily. And his boss worried only about whether the building would leak when it rained.

A lot of my work was practical. The Department worked all over the country. You get very interested in climate and rainfall and soils and winds. I made sure that my architects understood how important it was to build for the location and the climate.

NJ Your role was essentially safeguarding?

RP I wanted them to be excited about the work and the opportunities of government architecture. The new Brisbane airport was a good example of invention in architecture and construction. The Queensland office used a machine to roll out steel tray roofing on site—common now but not so then. The roof tapered and they rolled out the roof so that the trays got a fraction deeper and narrower at the gutter. All before computers. Clever and elegant.

It seemed right to me that the achievements of the Department ought to be recognised in a book about architecture and design. I worked with the regional offices to list completed buildings and landscapes and I made sure that everyone involved received due credit. Too often a project is written up in magazines as if the lead architect did every little bit and made the coffee as well. I made sure everyone who had played a part was named. Architecture can be a tough game. It helps if you can point to something and say I worked on that project. The Institute of Architects had started a series on the work of leading Australian architects and I plugged into that. The book was well received as part of the Institute series and as a bicentennial project for the Government.

NJ You were saying earlier that sometimes the Department did the early design work and handed it to a commercial office to document for construction.

RP That was a logical division of labour, we just couldn't maintain an office in each state to undertake every step of design and construction for every building. But in a sense it was the downfall of the Department. We were the principal architectural and engineering advisers to government. Frank and fearless and so on, the Chief Scientists and Chief Medical Officers of architecture. We gave the best advice, we were supposed to be the best informed. We had libraries that other architects couldn't afford. We had a big database physically and a corporate memory in our people that no one else had.

We had the capacity to find out what our client departments and agencies really wanted, how it was going to work, write the brief, get it costed, feasibility studies, concept designs. We were the best people to present the project before the Public Works Committee and we had expertise in all sorts of technical areas. When all this was worked out satisfactorily and the project had approval to proceed, we could call in a reputable private office to prepare working drawings and specifications.

But the rats in the ranks thought you could squash all this together. Economic rationalism, deregulation and free markets were suddenly the flavour of the decade. Why not go straight off to one of the larger firms who know a little bit about building jetties or runways and get them to do it all? Why build offices or laboratories when you can rent them on the open market? And that's what happened. It wasn't even death by a thousand cuts, it was instant execution, a guillotine.

NJ Was there no downsizing of the Department?

RP Well they had to downsize a little bit because you can't fire everybody at once. But there was no going back. Bits of the Department were hived off to other places. Managers can manage all this they said. There was a fellow in New Zealand called Roger Douglas who said drop everything that is not core government business. The rats had got together and that was that, the ship was going to sink.

Works and Housing wasn't a prestigious portfolio, it was a service portfolio. We contributed to policy but not to community issues of health or education or defence. We never had high profile ministers but we had some good thinkers like Chris Hurford. He was pretty alone in thinking it was the job of the government to house its own and build well.

NJ So what did the Commonwealth lose when it divested itself of a procurement capability?

RP What it no longer had was access to independent advice on issues of design and construction. No big idea thinking, no interest in

the best, not just the biggest or the cheapest. We all are affected by our built environment. But governments appear to do nothing to make it as good as it can be—no architectural agenda, the market will see to all that. Once upon a time we had a wonderful experimental building station which tested the materials and methods of our construction industries. Now we have cheap skins glued on to buildings and when they burn all the talk is about money.

Our cities are failing. They are expanding for private sector profit with no consideration of individual or community impact. Let's have a lot of houses over here, but I don't have to build a school do I, that's the government's job.

Should a government allow people to build really nasty places to live or work? We are talking about not having space to plant a tree but we know if there are no trees we will get no fresh air. A modern 21st century nation with all the resources and space in the world but big is beautiful, growth equals improvement, build more and more roads to nowhere, waste water.

NJ Australia has always been a very urbanised society but we appear to have little respect for or understanding of the built environment. The architectural community spends much time sampling the best urban environments in the world. We are more than capable of driving quality in our surroundings. Do

governments see this as not important enough to worry about?

RP Now we are into politics rather than design! Perhaps one day we will have cross-party agreement that our quality of life and the places where we live, work and play should be independent of electoral cycles and discussions about international trade. Perhaps there will be federal, state and local government consensus that good built environments are at the centre of everything. The question is not what does it cost but is it good and, most importantly, is it good enough?

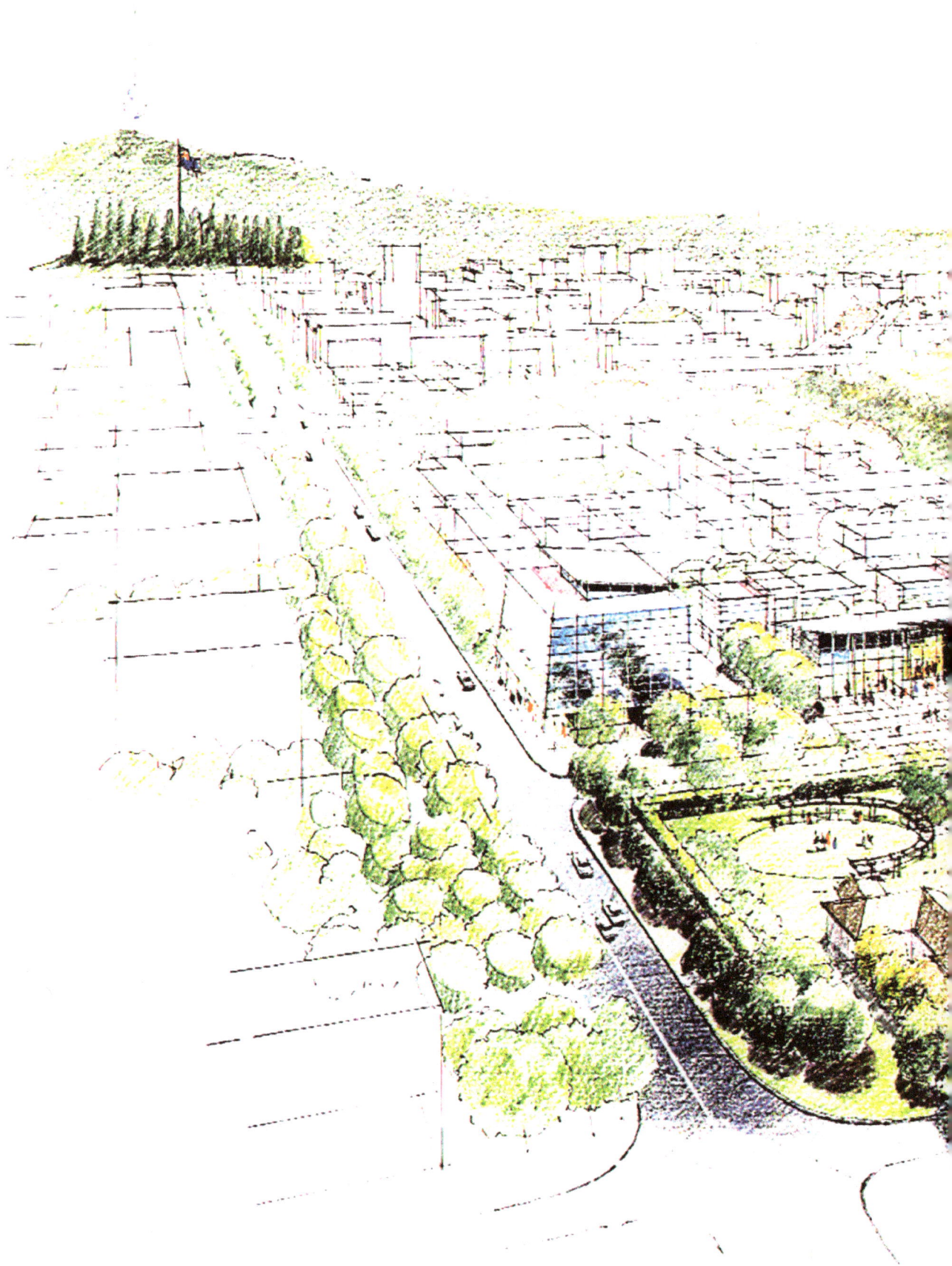

A Canberra Architecture

A Canberra Architecture

Nathan G Judd

Architecture in Canberra needs to offer both an interpretation of the city's short history and make a contribution to its future. These issues are perhaps more important for Canberra than for any other Australian city as Canberra has been only recently established. In this context, future opportunities can be degraded or erased and opportunities that would be treasured in other cities may be squandered .

Architecture in this city exists in the context of the Griffin plan/vision and subsequent overlay by planners, architects and authorities. Overall, the issues of scale, aesthetics, function and appropriate formal languages are critical in informing an architecture that reflects an idea or at the very least a knowledge of history of the Capital. Too many recent examples are basically imported models that are at worst merely suitable for indeterminate commercial office parks or are developed responses to other contexts and fail to grapple with the Griffin chassis as applied to the Canberra valley.

Roger Pegrum's work offers us an architecture developed here, that has grappled with this city for decades and is a mature language that fits its environment. It is at once urban in its conception, respectful of future opportunities and contributory to its meaning.

Romaldo Giurgola 1981

Anzac Parade 1963

Pegrum's first public place

The Griffin plan for Australia's national capital city responds directly to the landscape and topography of the Canberra valley. Griffin's major land axis runs southwest from Mount Ainslie to the distant Snowy Mountains and intersects with a water axis from Black Mountain along the line of an ornamental lake. Griffin reserved a site on his land axis at the foot of Mount Ainslie for a casino or pleasure garden for the people.

With the end of the First World War there was a national move to honour the more than 60,000 Australians who had lost their lives fighting for our freedom. Shrines and memorials were designed and built in all state capitals and in dozens of country towns and the Commonwealth government determined that there would be a national War Memorial in Canberra. The Mount Ainslie site was selected as 'pre-eminently the most suitable site that could be suggested for a building of the nature contemplated'. The Australian War Memorial was completed and opened to the public

in 1941 as one of a small number of fine public buildings in the new capital city.

In 1963, Pegrum was seconded from the Department of Works to the National Capital Development Commission to assist British architect Sir William Holford and his partner Richard Gray in the design of Anzac Parade, a major symbolic avenue from the Memorial to the lake then under construction. Pegrum was asked by Holford to suggest designs for the lights along the Parade and proposed slender hexagonal poles finished with a bronze finial and paired luminaires on long bronze arms at right angles.

The metaphor was clear—Australian and New Zealand soldiers faced each other as allies across the wide avenue with arms outstretched. The designs were warmly received by all parties and the lights were turned on by the Prime Minister Sir Robert Menzies on Anzac Day 1965, the 50th anniversary of the landing at Gallipoli. The original lighting was shown in a sketch of Anzac Parade by Romaldo Giurgola,

the winner of the 1980 competition for the design of the new and permanent Parliament House.

Pegrum's original lighting was replaced in 2000 with new energy efficient fittings of a similar design.

Old Parliament House 1965 - 67

Pegrum's second public place

What impresses one immediately in relation to the elegant portico that Roger designed while still a junior architect at the Department of Works, is the care with which it has been married to the original building and the simplicity and appropriateness of its expression. This portico is famously part of the backdrop for the Dismissal, the historical footage of Gough Whitlam is filmed with him standing beneath its canopy, creating a de facto stage for this dramatic moment in Australia's political history.

There is a fineness and care in the geometric columns welded up in plate steel but expressed in a masonry language and painted white to create a subtle relationship with the adjacent cement rendered lamp posts.

The fascia is expressed with shadow lines that tie it visually with the original building. The Commonwealth coat of arms is simply placed in the centre, on axis, and larger than the fascia. The ceiling has a margin between composed sheets, with expressed screws aligned with Griffin's land axis.

The portico is at a modest functional scale, but not double height nor a grand addition. The temptation must have been there for a young architect to make it a more prominent statement, but instead the response is measured, appropriate and respectful to the original building. Apart from a few coats of paint in the intervening fifty years, it has stood the test of time.

National Archives of Australia

Opening of Parliament, May 1927

11 November 1975

Governor-General's study

Chancery Government House Yarralumla 1994

In 1990 Pegrum was engaged to design a new Chancery building in the grounds of Government House Yarralumla. The Chancery houses the offices of the Governor-General and was opened by Prime Minister Paul Keating in 1993.

The Chancery follows many of the conventions of the Stripped Classical architectural style shared by other official buildings in Canberra and has been built to an exacting standard. The predominantly masonry language features horizontal shadow lines, pebbledash detailing with curved end walls with balcony terrace and steel framed windows within punched masonry openings. There is a formality to this building expressed in elements such as paired columns, the rhythm of the steel framed windows and the apparent simplicity of a compact working office building.

The interiors express a real beauty in their detailing which is both traditional and contemporary. A modern insitu concrete blade wall is complemented with a decidedly modern glass skylight and concrete columns punctuate the

Brett Boardman

space. This is contrasted with the main terrazzo staircase complete with stringer and carpet runner secured with stainless stair rods. Fine timber detailing is evident in stepped skirtings and architraves, timber doors and timber panelling to meeting rooms and offices.

The building transcends the limitations of economy and appropriateness demanded of a public building. Programmatic opportunities such as circulation are accommodated within a gallery, general public spaces connect visually both vertically and horizontally, transparency and view corridors are accommodated without overt deference. Ceiling heights are employed as a hierarchical device and the adjacent view relationship to the lake is all resolved in an expert manner.

Ben Wrigley

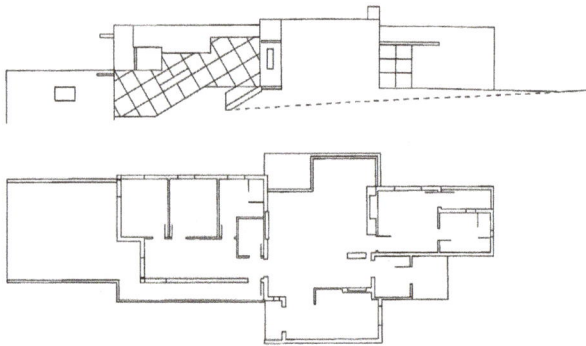

Morris House Yarralumla 2003

Commendation, Institute of Architects, 2003

As Canberra matured, a reimagining of the inner suburbs began and old housing stock was slowly replaced, generally with larger unremarkable dwellings. In this instance a client who already lived in an architect designed house chose to downsize in Yarralumla.

Musgrave Street is a long narrow street which was developed in the late 1940s with government cottages and semi-detached houses in brick and weatherboard. Continuous verge plantings of mature Chinese elms make it one of the most attractive streets in this inner Canberra suburb.

The Morris House replaced a 1950s semi-detached house with a contemporary energy efficient light filled townhouse perfectly calibrated for the occupant. The house is organised to suit a single person with main bedroom, bathroom and private walled courtyard fronting the street, a central main living area and kitchen with northern aspect opening onto a small sunny terrace, and a separate visitors wing with generous bedrooms, rumpus room and stair access to wine cellar and basement parking. This planning approach of inverting the requirements of a traditional family home allows parts of the house to lay dormant until required. This approach was to be later employed in the Reid House

The external materiality of the house is of boxy white painted brick volumes, white framed double glazing and white painted steelwork. This restrained material palette is perfectly at home in the consular suburb of Yarralumla, where many embassy buildings employ a similar building language.

The interiors feature a similar restrained use of materials, with honey coloured Victorian ash floors, white kitchen joinery with blue accent splashback, white painted walls and ceiling and integrated Victorian ash joinery.

Turner Apartments 2003

ACT Government High Quality Sustainable Design Award, 2004

Master Builders Association Excellence in Building Award, 2004

Housing Industry Association Apartment Building of the Year Award, 2004

For Canberra architects there is often a sense of being either within or outside Griffin's plan, the town's 'City Walls' so to speak. This apartment project by Roger is firmly within the City Walls in Macleay Street, Turner.

Macleay Street appears on Griffin's earliest plans for Canberra and is one of the most attractive streets in the central areas of the city. Continuous street plantings of mature oak trees link the street to Haig Park, Charles Weston's wonderful green 'city wall'. At the south end is Ken Woolley's Seventh Day Adventist church and the adjacent Lutheran National Memorial church by Frederick Romberg

The Turner apartments have a balanced asymmetrical low scale art deco feel befitting its inner Canberra location. The building offers a sense of quality and solidity though its materiality and detailing.

The rendered brickwork construction has allowed Roger to emphasise punched window openings and curved masonry balconies and employ a stepped parapet and floor plan to express depth and volume in the façade.

The simplicity of the soft grey masonry colour palette is accented with pastel accents. Stepped shadow lines in the balconies emphasise the horizontal. A sense of detail and complexity is introduced via steelwork in balustrade and pergola elements and subtlety in the glazing design. These elements in combination create interest and rhythm and contribute to the attractive streetscape.

Macleay Street

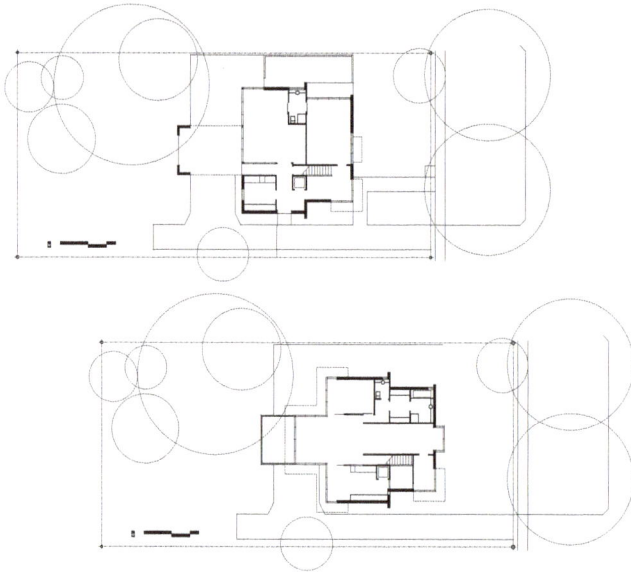

Matt Kelso

Reid House 2005

Canberra Medallion, Institute of Architects, 2006

In 2004, empty-nesters Roger and Annabelle chose to reimagine their housing and parted company with their sprawling 1927 Oakley and Parkes designed house in Forrest.

The Reid house addressed a new brief; living as a couple in the inner north of the city, incorporating an architectural studio and guest quarters. The almost Manor House model organises living areas for the couple at first floor engaging with the treescape and views to the city. This first floor living level is arrived at via stairs from a spacious foyer that allows access to both the guest suite and the architectural studio. This programmatic approach resolves issues of building address and security and encourages future flexibility as needs change over time.

The building presents a double storey red dry pressed brick façade to the street offering a contextual nod to the adjacent built context. This is teamed with steel framed windows, a popped window box and lightweight cladding and render. The building demonstrates a restrained use of steel construction and detailing and offers a sense of transparency and activity to the street.

Within the house there is a consistency of forms and finishes with double height spaces and generous daylight. Feature steel framed glazed walls define security and privacy with glazing that extends the eye and allows for porosity between spaces.

100
CANBERRA
HOUSES
A Century of
Capital
Architecture

Tim Reeves &
Alan Roberts

Ben Wrigley

A Professional Opinion

Mads Gaardboe

I first met Roger on Stonehaven Crescent Deakin, in Annabelle's living room—which that day was the venue for a meeting of a newly established working group of some of Canberra's practising architects. To the west we had picturesque views over Deakin's treetops to Black Mountain and opposite, through the kitchen window, children's heads appeared with regularity: Lissy and Luke were jumping on the trampoline.

Roger arrived and was introduced. There was little doubt that Annabelle, by persuading him to join her team, had secured a scoop. I was a relative newcomer to Australia's architectural scene but I was certainly aware of Roger's reputation—as the Government Architect of course, but also for a raft of buildings and for his articulate views on architecture and planning in Canberra and elsewhere. I was working in the National Capital Development Commission at the time and I might have been encouraged, mischievously perhaps, to feel that Roger was regarded by our Chief Architect as the ultimate challenger to being the Alpha Architect in town. And if Greg had that concern, it would have been entirely understandable.

Roger's past in renowned English architectural offices and an academic career in Sydney undoubtedly provided wider perspective to his observations and opinions than most could claim. Yet, above all, Roger's architectural commitment has predominantly been to the Canberra discourse and his joining our little working group was a case in point. Where he can see an opportunity to encourage architectural debate, he is a generous contributor.

Few architects have been vocal on as many levels as Roger. Many architectural critics tend to focus on interpretation, others on descriptive assessment of built projects. Roger, seemingly effortlessly, bridges the two, often completing the story by adding biographical information and references to political context and the environment. His articles do not adhere to conventional narrow subjects for specialist readers, but address a large audience on many subjects. This is not done in a casual or ad-hoc way, there is a discernable underlying ethical coherence and genuine passion behind his publications that demands attention.

Roger is a prolific author and commentator on all aspects of our built environment, new and old, architectural or urban, through biographies, monographs, book reviews, jury reports and interviews. I recall his critical distress, professed over a cup of coffee—or was it a glass of wine?—at Canberra's then predilection for largely introverted buildings in Civic; the bigger the better, it seemed. Believing that such opinions are limited to private conversations is to underestimate his appetite for outspoken (but always civil) castigation of misguided or insensitive developments.

And of course there are some seminal publications we all are familiar with. His two volumes of *Details in Australian Architecture* I particularly remember from my early years teaching at the University of Canberra: a real inspiration for students to understand that good architectural design penetrates deep into the construction detail. The other is one of my all-time favourites—*The Bush Capital*. Without it, my own appreciation of Canberra's history and research of aspects thereof would not have developed as it did. It is packed with information that is made easily digestible by professionals and laypeople alike, peppered with original illustrations, amusing anecdotes and perceptive interpretations of unfolding events. It helps educate us—the community at large—to admire our capital city's heritage. It would have been seriously remiss not to have been re-printed 30 years after its first publication as part of Canberra's centenary celebrations.

Last—but not least—Roger's buildings. Look in the real estate papers and it is rare that the architect's name is mentioned. However, if it is a Roger Pegrum house, it often is. His own house is a case in point. Modern yes, but sitting comfortably in the historic suburb of Reid, it is deservedly recognised by his peers. The plan allows for flexible uses downstairs. When visiting, my family (Sue, Martin, Pia and Finn) always comment on the bountiful natural light filling the first floor, the crisp detailing and the splashes of red framing that define the different spaces in a mostly open plan. Beautiful indeed.

Among many other buildings Roger has designed, I particularly remember two: the Chancery at Government House, with its meticulous detailing—window framing crafted with historic reference etc.—and the Faculty of Asian Studies at the Australian National University. At the time I was member of the Buildings and Grounds Committee at the ANU. The University could undoubtedly be a testing client (the reference to the façade's 3 Y's did not amuse Roger I think), but his building deserves its place with the iconic School of Art and the School of Music, and while finishing the edge of the crescent, it also creates a distinctive tie between the Baldessin Precinct and the rest of the campus.

Roger is a rare breed of architect these days, where narrow specialisation is what defines so many others. He is, I will suggest, the true renaissance man, and our profession—and the community—have long been, and still very much are, the beneficiaries.

EDDIE GONZALEZ
JUNI 00

List of Works

List of Works

Selected Projects

**Commonwealth Department of Works
1961-1968**

1962

Woden Valley Primary and Infants Schools
Hughes, Garran, Lyons and Mawson

Visitor Centre at Tidbinbilla Nature Reserve
(destroyed in bushfires January 2003)

1963

Anzac Parade Light Fittings (with Sir William Holford)

Private Practice 1968-1974
(with Anthony Pegrum 1968-1971)

Walker House

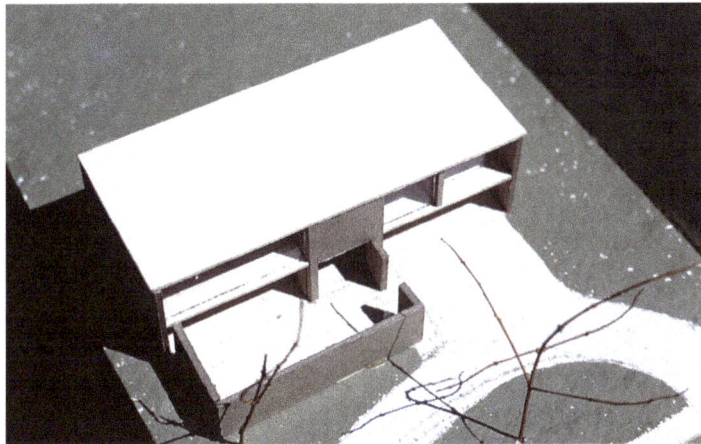

Ryan House

Lewis House

1963

Walker House, 43 Cobby Street Campbell

1968

Ryan House, 58 Rosenthal Street Campbell
Lewis House, 34 Tompson Street Garran
Sautelle House, 19 Richardson Street Garran
Conan-Davies House, 28 Araba Street Aranda
Pegrum House 1, 16 Stone Place Garran
Kluken House 1, 10 Janari Place Aranda
Hickson House, 86 Pridham Street Farrer

1969

Gloucester Park Golf Course Narrabundah
Shell Depot, Ipswich Street Fyshwick
Children's Day Nursery, Robson Street Garran
Hardy House, 6 Marawa Place Aranda
Barratt House, 47 Skinner Street Cook
Crawford House, 29 Shackleton Circuit Mawson

Slee/Harris House

1970

Slee/Harris House, 29 Waite Street Farrer
Lowrey House, the Ridgeway Queanbeyan NSW
Braddick House, 13 Gidabal Street Aranda
MacDonald House, 8 Moss Street Cook
Macdonald House, 46 Mirning Crescent Aranda
Kimpton House, 18 Araba Place Aranda ACT
Falk House, 20 Araba Place Aranda ACT
Four project houses, 5-11 Hoseason Street Mawson
(and elsewhere as Manor Homes)

Manor house

1971

Chancery at Japanese Embassy Yarralumla
(in association with T Sakamaki and
Japan Department of Works)

Boldeman House, 17 Woodgate Street Farrer

Milne House, 34 Esperance Street Red Hill

Wight House, 42 Rapanea Street Rivett

Lancaster House, 5 Steinwedel Street Farrer

McKeown House, 35 Mirning Crescent Aranda

Archer House, Downes Place Hughes

Police guard boxes various embassies and
the Prime Minister's Lodge

Chancery Japanese Embassy

Boldeman House

Police guard boxes Prime Minister's Lodge

Wight House

Lancaster House

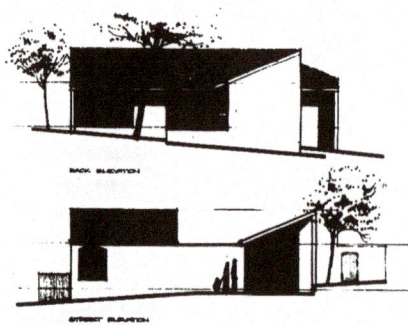

MCKEOWN HOUSE

1972

Mini Centres Kambah and Wanniassa
(for National Capital Development Commission)
Price House, 107 Gouger Street Torrens
Five townhouses 3-11 Rymill Place Mawson
Schoefl/Miles House, Sutton NSW
Cumpston House, 42 Araba Street Aranda

Price House

Rymill Place

Nick Burrows

Byam Wight

Cumpston House

1973

Kemp House 41 Pelham Close Chapman
(destroyed in bushfires January 2003)

Hunt House, Merindah Avenue Moree NSW

Diener House, 39 McEachern Street Melba

25 Aged Persons' Units, Gilmore Crescent Garran
[demolished 2016]

Kluken House 2, Bluegum Place Roseville NSW

Maher House, 15 Marrakai Street Hawker

Walker House, 31 Ambalindum Street Hawker

Carter House, 55 Brereton Street Garran

Wilson House, 38 Mirning Crescent Aranda

*RAIA CS Daley Medal 1974, RAIA 25-Year award
2006, RAIA Commendation for bathroom refurbishment
and MBA Bathroom of the Year 2014*

Condomaxium prefabricated housing (Project)

Maher House

Wilson House

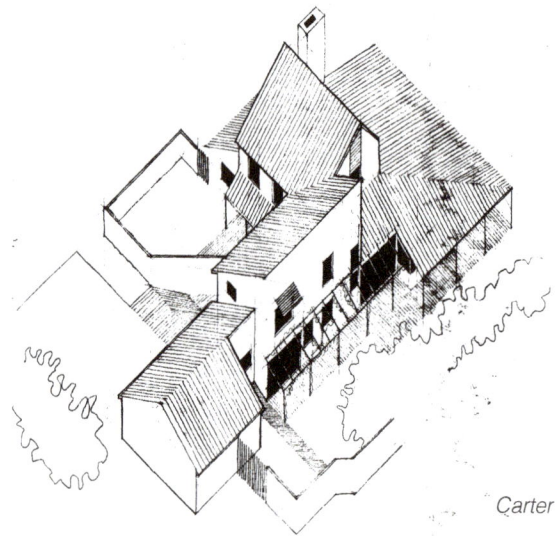

Carter House

Condomaxium prefabricated housing

1977

Reserve Bank NSW Training College Kirribili, Conservation Study

Entry to United Nations Habitat Competition for the Urban Environment of Developing Countries focused on Manila (del Paul Pholeros)

**Jackson Teece Chesterman Willis
1989**

1989

First prize: Urban Design Competition for City Hill sponsored by ACT Planning Authority, National Capital Planning Authority and Royal Australian Institute of Architects

First prize: Urban Design Competition for Sydney Showground sponsored by NSW Government and Royal Australian Planning Institute

THE·CITY·GARDENS·

**Jackson Teece Chesterman Willis
1990-1991**

Faculty of Education at the University of Sydney
First prize in invited competition

St Clare's College

Pegrum/Ciolek Architects 1992-1994

1992

Gymnasium and Dance Studios, St Clare's College Griffith

Pentony House, Gooroomon Ponds Road Hall NSW
MBA Excellence in Building Award 1992

Pentony House

Primary and Infants School, Gordon ACT
RAIA Award of Merit 1993

24 Garden Flats Theodore ACT
MBA Excellence in Building Award 1994

Canberra Cultural and Heritage Centre
Feasibility Study

Perth City Foreshore
Urban Design Competition

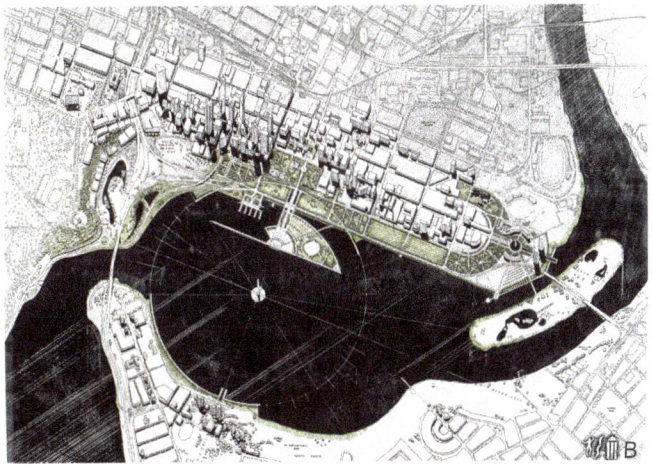

Perth City Foreshore

1993

Faculty of Asian Studies at the Australian National University
First prize invited competition

Lanyon High School

Lanyon High School

1994

Chancery at Government House
First prize invited competition

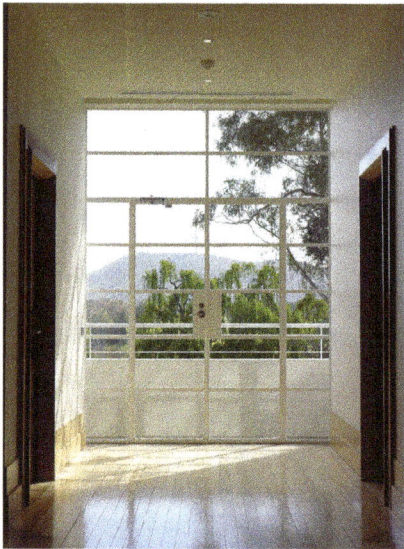

Brett Boardman

From the Chancery towards Black Mt

Pegrum and Associates
1995 -

1995

Heritage management plans:
Patent Office, Edmund Barton Building,
University House, St Christopher's School
and Convent

Therapeutic Goods Administration
Symonston ACT
First prize in invited competition
MBA Excellence in Building Award 1997

1996

Vice-Chancellor's Residence at
the University of Canberra—Invited
competition

1997

National Museum of Australia Acton and
Australian Institute of Aboriginal and
Torres Strait Islander Studies.
Functional brief for design competition

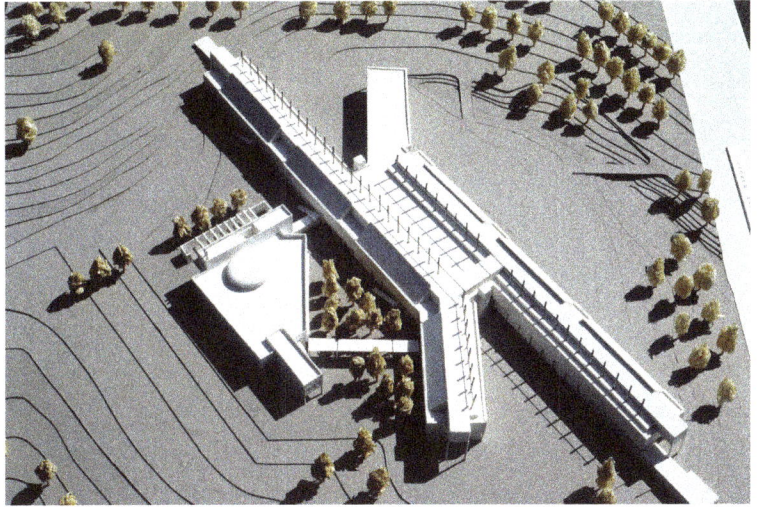

Therapeutic Goods Administration

Vice-Chancellor's Residence, University of Canberra

1999 -

Calvary Clinic Specialist Medical Centre, Bruce
MBA Excellence in Building Award 2001

ACTTAB Headquarters Dickson
First prize in invited competition

Kintore Crescent Townhouses

Catholic Education Office, Franklin Street
Manuka
MBA Excellence in Building Award 2001

Eight Townhouses, Kintore Crescent
Yarralumla
ACT Government High Quality Sustainable
Design Award 2001

Seven Townhouses, Hartigan Street Garran

Botany and Zoology
Australian National University–
invited competition

Australian National University
Refurbishment of University House

Botany and Zoology ANU

University House ANU

THE MELBOURNE BUILDING
SPECIFICATION: EXTERNAL PAINT COLOURS
PAINT COLOUR SCHEDULE - ELEVATION 1
22 April 1998

Pegrum
Associates

Melbourne Building refurbishment,
West Row Canberra City
Property Council of Australia Rider
Hunt Award for Excellence and
Innovation 2001

Centre for Arab and Islamic Studies at
The Australian National University—
Invited competition

Morris House, 25 Musgrave Street
Yarralumla
RAIA Commendation and Master
Builders Association Excellence in
Building Award 2003

Dobinson's Bakery, Bunda St,
Canberra City

Fooks House, 40 Monkman Street
Chapman

Grandstand and player facilities,
Belconnen Soccer Club Mackellar
RAIA Commendation 2003

Lasek Ekelund House, 23 Monkman
Street Chapman

Belconnen Aquatic Centre, Eastern
Valley Way Belconnen (project)

Macleay Street Apartments, 8 Macleay
Street Turner
ACT Government High Quality
Sustainable Design Award 2003

MBA Excellence in Building Award
2004

Housing Industry Association
Apartment Building of the Year 2004

Pitt/O'Dea House, 73 Limestone
Avenue Braddon

Paul/Webb House, Braddon

Pegrum House 2, 19 Euree Street Reid
RAIA Canberra Medallion 2006

St John's Church, Reid
Commendation
Urban Design Competition

Fraser Court Redevelopment, Kingston

Dobinsons and Nutmeg Concession,
Canberra Centre

Publications

'They raised the ceiling', *The Australian*, 14 June 1965

'Cedar on stark white: the Lewis House', *The Canberra Times*, 21 March 1967

'New office and amenities building at Canberra', *Shell Times*, July 1968

'A smaller house with courtyard', Ann Whitelaw, *The Canberra Times*, 12 March 1968

'Splendid view across timbered hills', Ann Whitelaw, *The Canberra Times*, 13 August 1968

'Warm, friendly and comfortable house with courtyard', Ann Whitelaw, *The Canberra Times*, 18 June 1968

'Plywood and timber used lavishly', Ann Whitelaw, *The Canberra Times*, 14 January 1969

'Charm of the open fire', Roger Pegrum, *The Canberra Times*, 7 March 1969

'The search for an elusive soul', Roger Pegrum, *The Canberra Times*, 11 March 1969

'A 'small fortress' on a corner: 14 squares of privacy', Ann Whitelaw, *The Canberra Times*, 3 June 1969

'Small home in a perfect setting', Ann Whitelaw, *The Canberra Times*, 7 October 1969

'Two of the latest homes from Canberra architects Roger and Anthony Pegrum', *Cross-Section*, University of Melbourne Department of Architecture, December 1969

'A split level roof makes an interesting house', Ann Whitelaw, *The Canberra Times*, 17 March 1970

'High-rise comes to Queanbeyan', *The Queanbeyan Age*, 17 April 1970

'Phoenix group has grown for 187 years', *Canberra News*, 18 November 1970

'Clinker brick home', Ann Whitelaw, *The Canberra Times*, 26 May 1970

'A breakaway in Canberra: new homes shake off the formality', Eric Wilson, *The Australian Home Beautiful*, August 1970

'Display suddenly important', *The Canberra Times*, 12 February 1973

'Making a little go a long way', Eric Wilson, *Home Beautiful*, April 1971

'Canberra's Architecture', Roger Pegrum, *The Canberra Times*, 25 September 1970

'Sign Language', Roger Pegrum, *The Canberra Times*, 19 June 1970

'Bricks take on second life', Ann Blight, *The Canberra Times*, 11 June 1971

'Natural finish and triangular', Ann Whitelaw, *The Canberra Times*, 4 August 1970

'Exhilarating new ideas', Doreen Hungerford, *The Canberra Times*, 29 June 1971

'The problems of the new towns: the Canberra concept British style', Roger Pegrum, *The Canberra Times*, 14 June 1971

'Taking the trauma out of shopping', Roger Pegrum, *The Canberra Times*, 18 October 1971

'Keep Work Here: Planner', *Canberra News*, 1 October 1971

'Capital roundabout', Roger Pegrum, *The Australian*, 29 October 1971

'Building-in a sense of theatre', Roger Pegrum, *The Australian*, 19 November 1971

'Designing for Science', Roger Pegrum, *The Australian*, 10 December 1971

'An experiment with space', Roger Pegrum, *The Australian*, 3 March 1972

'The brothers Pegrum', Leonie Woolley, *Australian Home Journal*, April 1972

'Swinger Hill erupts again', *Canberra Sunday Post*, 27 February 1972

'The Yellow Submarine: Mystery TAB', *Canberra News*, 24 August 1972

'Environment—Ski fields can easily be destroyed', Roger Pegrum, *Australian Skiing News*, 26 May 1972

'Thredbo—a village in a magical setting', Roger Pegrum, *Australian Skiing News*, 9 June 1972

'More simplicity needed in resort buildings', Roger Pegrum, *Australian Skiing News*, 7 July 1972

'East-West go south for the snow', Roger Pegrum, *Australian Skiing News*, 4 August 1972

'Police get guard boxes', *The Canberra Times*, 25 September 1972

'Liberty's price: eternal vigilance', *The Australian*, 26 September 1972

'Kindergarten and Day Nursery', *Architecture in Australia*, October 1972

'The Year of 45', Roger Pegrum, *The Canberra Times*, 6 January 1973

'Conan-Davies House', *Architecture in Australia*, February 1973

'A modern corner store for Kambah', *Canberra News*, 22 August 1973

'Canberra: a company town', Roger Pegrum,, *The Canberra Times*, 26 September 1973

'Garran home units for the elderly', *The Canberra Times*, 21 November 1973

'Scholarship winner: Roger Pegrum', *BNIA* November/December 1973

'Looking into the problems of growing old', Roger Pegrum, *The Canberra Times*, 24 December 1973

'Total care of the aged in today's society', Ann Dalgarno, *The Canberra Times*, 3 January 1974

'Reviewing ACT architecture in 1973', Roger Pegrum, *The Canberra Times*, 14 January 1974

'Housing: Dream or Reality', *Current Politics*, 1974

'O'Malley described as a disaster', Graeme O'Neill, *The Canberra News*, 27 March 1974

'Building 'lagged in technical innovation'', *The Canberra Times*, 1 April 1974

'Thoughts on the new ACT seat: the big split'', Roger Pegrum, *The Canberra Times*, 2 May 1974

'Country charm and comfort in city style', *The Sun-Herald*, 8 December 1974

'Doctor's house at Aranda', *The Canberra Times*, 19 December 1974

'Wot, no wardens on the catwalks?', Roger Pegrum, *Architecture in Australia*, August 1975

'Home Units, Berry's Bay', Roger Pegrum, Architecture in Australia, October 1975

'Forgotten people factor', Roger Pegrum, a review of *Cities for Sale* by Leone Sandercock, *The Sydney Morning Herald*, 24 January 1976

Provisional Parliament House Canberra: Conservation Management Plan, R Pegrum with H Tanner and M Kelly, 1976

The Architecture of Old Age: Housing for the Active Elderly, Roger Pegrum, HAL Scholarship, RAIA, 1976

'Our dirty, disorderly, desolate cities', Roger Pegrum, a review of *Urban Development in Australia* by Max Neutze, *The Australian*, 7 May 1977

'Politicians and aesthetics', Roger Pegrum, *The Australian*, 19 May 1977

'The genius no one ever understood', Roger Pegrum, a review of *The Architecture of Walter Burley Griffin* by Donald Leslie Johnson, *The Australian*, 27 May 1977

'A ray of hope for our cities', Roger Pegrum, a review of *How Cities are Saved* by Herbert Lottman, *The Australian*, 1 August 1977

'The Job for a Genius', Roger Pegrum, *The Weekend Australian Magazine*, 20-21 August 1977

'The House that Barry built', Roger Pegrum, a review of *Mid-Victorian Masterpiece* by Barnett Cocks, *The Australian*, 2 September 1977

'A is for 'Arry Seidler', Roger Pegrum', a review of *Who's Who in Architecture* by J M Richards, *The Australian*, 17 October 1977

'Roles of Guardians, Improvers', Roger Pegrum, a review of *Environmental Management in Australia*, by J M Powell, *The Canberra Times*, 29 October 1977

'Face to face with the fenceless society', Roger Pegrum, *The Weekend Australian*, 5-6 November 1977

'Antipodean palaces', Roger Pegrum, a review of *Historic Buildings of Australia*, National Trust, *The Australian*, 7 November 1977

'A fearful mob of ringbarkers', Roger Pegrum, *The Weekend Australian Magazine*, 31 December-1 January 1977/78

'Freewheeling through a Woollahra celebration', *The Sydney Morning Herald* , 5 August 1978

'Language and architecture', Roger Pegrum, a review of *The Modern Language of Architecture* by Bruno Zevi, *24 Hours*, November 1978

'UN Habitat Competition Manila: Roger Pegrum' in *The Architecture of Self-Help Communities*, ed Michael Seelig, McGraw Hill 1978

'The Bastakia of Dubai'; 'Hello Abu Dhabi and Dubai', Roger Pegrum, *Cathay Pacific Discovery*, 1978

'Daryl Jackson', Roger Pegrum, entry in *Contemporary Architects*, ed Muriel Emmanuel, Macmillan 1979

'Landscapes of social relevance', Roger Pegrum, a review of *Park Maker: a life of Frederick Law Olmstead* by Elizabeth Stevenson, *The Weekend Australian Magazine*, 26-27 May 1979

'Two books about Sydney and how the city grew', Roger Pegrum, reviews of *Sydney takes shape* by Max Kelly and Ruth Crocker and *Sydney since the Twenties* by Peter Spearritt, *24 Hours*, May 1979

'Plan for a People City', Roger Pegrum, a review of *The Green City* by Roger Johnson, *24 Hours*, May 1979

'Newsweek theme on Dubai businessmen', *The Gulf News*, 9 September 1980

'Substantial and Serious', Roger Pegrum, a review of *The Victorian Country House* by Mark Girouard, *Quadrant*, November 1980

'Players in the game of society', Roger Pegrum, *POL*, 1980

'Adelaide's Architectural Watchdog: Robert Dickson', Roger Pegrum, *POL*, Holiday Issue 1980 81

'A Frozen Moment in a Short History', Roger Pegrum, *POL*, February 1981

'Some thoughts on the 1981 Merit Awards', Roger Pegrum, *Architecture Bulletin,* 1981

'A quest for relevance: Peter Corrigan and Maggie Edmond', Roger Pegrum, *POL*, April-May 1981

'The Old Walls Around us', Roger Pegrum, a review of *The Open-Air Museum* by D N Jeans and Peter Spearritt, *Quadrant*, December 1981

'Two-Wheeled Contraception', Roger Pegrum, a review of *The Bicycle and the Bush* by Jim Fitzpatrick, *Quadrant*, April 1982

'Living Cheek to Cheek', Roger Pegrum, a review of *Medium Density Housing in Australia* eds Bruce Judd and John Dean, RAIA, in J*ournal of Architectural and Planning Research*, New York, July 1982

'Hierophants and Apostates and other Architects', Roger Pegrum, a review of *From Bauhaus to Our House* by Tom Wolfe, *Quadrant*, October 1982

'*Dwellings for the Elderly: a Design Guide*' by Juanita Neale Saxby, reviewed by Roger Pegrum, *Architecture Australia*, November 1982

'A room with a view: the Madonna Inn', Roger Pegrum, *POL*, August 1983

The Bush Capital: How Australia chose Canberra as its Federal City, Roger Pegrum, Hale and Iremonger, 1983; second edition Watermark Press, 2008

Reviews of *The Bush Capital*:

    George Temperley, *Canberra Historical Journal*, March 1983

    'Some boobs', *The Sun-Herald*, 13 February 1983

    'A village that just missed the spotlight', Philip Derriman, *The Sydney Morning Herald*, 10 March 1983

    'How the city of wagging tongues found a site', Steve Harris, *The Age*, 11 March 1983

    'Fights and birth pains of our bush capital', Alex Kennedy, *The Advertiser*, 12 March 1983

    'Capital book launched', *The Canberra Times*, 13 March,1983

    'Capital 'stolen' from the sheep', Nick Yardley, *The Sun-Herald*, 27 March 1983

    'The Bush Capital: some juicy chapters', *The University of Sydney News*, 29 March 1983

    'Canberra: a beginning in wisdom', Manning Clark, *The National Times*, 25-31 March 1983

    'Canberra's full story still to come', Hope Hewitt, *The Canberra Times*, 16 April 1983

    'Parochial politics urbanified', Ken Scully, *The Catholic Weekly*, 27 April,1983

    'The road to the Bush Capital', Edmund Campion, *The Bulletin*, 17 May 1983

    'Canberra—the result of years of sordid bickering', Bernard Campbell, *The West Australian*, 21 May 1983

    'First political squabble was about Canberra', Cliff Cranfield, *The Newcastle Herald*, 21 May 1983

    'How Australia chose Canberra as its Federal City', John Minnery, *Architecture Australia*, September 1983

    'Faltering Steps Towards Nationhood', Edward St John, *Quadrant*, October 1983

'die Geschichte der Gruendung und Entstehung der australischen Hauptstadt Canberra', *Garten und Landschaft*, Zeitschrift der Deutschen Gesellschaft fuer Gartenkunst und Landschaftspflege 9/83

'Griffin is dead! Long live Griffin!', Roger Pegrum, *Architecture Australia*, September 1983

Details in Australian Architecture, Roger Pegrum, RAIA 1984, reprinted 1987; Details in Australian Architecture vol II, RAIA 1987

'Mitchell/Giurgola Architects', a review by Roger Pegrum, *Architecture Australia*, November 1984

'From Tocal to Yulara' in *Australian Architects: Philip Cox*, RAIA 1984

'From Yulara to Darling Harbour' in *Australian Architects: Philip Cox Richardson Taylor and Partners*, RAIA 1988

'The Mother Test', Roger Pegrum, a review of *Leslie Wilkinson: A Practical Idealist* by Susanne Falkiner; *Architecture for the New World: The Work of Harry Seidler* by Peter Blake; and *John Andrews: Architecture a Performing Art* by Jennifer Taylor, *Architecture in Australia*, April 1985

Details in Australian Architecture, Roger Pegrum, reviewed by Graham Holland, *Architecture Australia*, May 1985

'The architecture of Bruce Eeles', Roger Pegrum, *Architecture Australia*, May 1985

Australian Government Architects, RAIA/AGPS, 1988

'Canberra' in *The Origin of Australia's Capital Cities*, ed P Statham OUP 1988

'Art Deco Excitements', Roger Pegrum, a review of *In the Deco Style* by Dan Klein, *Quadrant*, June 1988

'Piers, Trams and Cafes to Revive a City's Heart', Christine Salins, *The Canberra Times* 10 May 1989

'Shemozzle City doesn't know where it is going', Harry Robinson, *The Sydney Morning Herald*, 15 May 1989

'New plan for Canberra city', *Architecture Australia*, June 1989

'New design plans for old Civic', Roger Pegrum, *Australian Financial Review*, 29 June 1989

'$10.5m to revamp theatre centre', Robert Macklin, *The Canberra Times*, 8 October 1989

'A city gardens plan for the showground', Geraldine O'Brien, *The Sydney Morning Herald*, 17 November 1989

'Quality Down Under' in *Building Evaluation: Advances in Methods and Applications*, Roger Pegrum with Peter Bycroft, ed W F E Preiser, Plenum Publishing, New York, 1990

'Success for Canberra architects', Philip Hobbs, *The Canberra Times*, 24 November 1989

'Changing face of City Hill', David Sibley, *The Canberra Times*, 19 August 1992

'Gordon school among top designs', David Sibley, *The Valley View*, 14 July 1993

'ACT Architecture week', David Sibley, *The Canberra Times*, 11 July 1993

'Tickets, please...for the heritage register', Michael Bachelard, *The Canberra Times*, 1 September 1994

'Your taxes at work, behind closed doors', Aban Contractor, *The Canberra Times*, 12 August 1995

'It is the very model for a modern Governor-General', Robert Macklin, *The Canberra Times*, 15 August 1995

'Logging on to the future', Verona Burgess, *The Canberra Times*, 9 March 1996

'Baldessin', in *Buildings and Landscapes: The Australian National University*, J Banks and M Gaardboe, ANU 1996

'Hovering disc not aliens', *The Canberra Times*, 22 September 1996

'New Symonston office has all the angles', Graham Cooke, *The Canberra Times*, 26 November 1996

'Irish pub and restaurants for Melbourne Building', Graham Cooke, *The Canberra Times*, 5 November 1997

'The schools that Canberra built', Verona Burgess, *The Canberra Times*, 7 March 1998

'Eat, drink and be merry in Civic', Norman Abjorensen, *Panorama*, 27 February 1999

'Kenneth Henry Oliphant' in *Australian Dictionary of Biography*, 1999 and 'Cuthbert Claude Mortier Whitley' in *Australian Dictionary of Biography*, 2003

'From first to last, chief architect's views of the city: the man behind the monuments', Frank Cassidy, *The Canberra Times*, 25 January 2000

'Melbourne Building receives property honour', Graham Cooke, *The Canberra Times*, 17 June 2000

'Take a break at Bunda Street bakery sidewalk of style', Christine Salins, *The Canberra Times*, 20 December 2000

'Homing in on the top end of the property market', Graham Cooke, *The Canberra Times*, 8 May 2001

'Griffith site pivotal to Griffin's plan', Roger Pegrum, *The Canberra Times*, 5 June 2001

'Give the public what it wants', Roger Pegrum, a review of *The Look of Architecture* by Witold Rybczynski, *The Canberra Times*, August 2001

'The Canberra Experiment', Roger Pegrum, *The Washington Times: The World and I*, October 2001

'A modern redesign', *The Canberra Sunday Times*, 29 June 2003

'A sporting standout', *The Canberra Sunday Times*, 27 July 2003

'Avoiding the clichés', *The Canberra Times*, 19 September 2004

'Finally we get a peek at Kintore', Graham Cooke, *The Canberra Sunday Times*, 19 September 2004

'*The Dream of a dreamer*', Roger Pegrum, Introduction to *Canberra Architecture* by Andrew Metcalf, The Watermark Press 2003

'Reid House', *The Canberra Times*, 15 June 2006

'At home ... among the trees', Karen Hardy, *The Canberra Times*, 13 July 2006

'Secret garden unique design unto itself', Peter Colquhoun, *Better Homes and Gardens*, November 2006

'Presenting one of our better homes', Carla Rocavert, *The Canberra Times*, 20 September 2006

'A window into Griffin's mind', Roger Pegrum, a review of *The Writings of Walter Burley Griffin*, ed Dustin Griffin, *The Canberra Times*, 7 June 2008

'From suburb slums to millionaires' row', John Thistleton, *The Canberra Times*, 10 March 2009

'Walter and Marion, true to the creative vocation', Roger Pegrum, a review of *Grand Obsessions: The Life and Work of Walter Burley Griffin and Marion Mahony Griffin* by Alasdair McGregor, *The Canberra Times*, 3 October 2009

'A history of the Australian Academy of Science', Roger Pegrum, speech at the launch of *A Big, Bold, Simple Concept* by Alan Roberts, Academy of Science Canberra, 27 April 2000, published as a book review in *Canberra Historical Journal*, May 2010

'Ainslie tree removal act of vandalism', Breanna Tucker, *The Canberra Times*, 27 October 2010

Addicted to Architecture, Robert Dickson, Wakefield Press, 2010

'The Australian Quarter Acre Block', Roger Pegrum, Manning Clark House Weekend of Ideas, *National Museum of Australia*, April 2011

'Robert Charles Given Coulter' and 'National Capital Development Commission', Roger Pegrum, in *Encyclopedia of Australian Architecture*, eds Philip Goad and Julie Willis, Cambridge University Press, 2011

'Roger Pegrum', by Ken Charlton, in *Encyclopedia of Australian Architecture*, eds Philip Goad and Julie Willis, Cambridge University Press, 2011

'Pegrum House' in *100 Canberra Houses: A Century of Capital Architecture*, Tim Reeves and Alan Roberts, Halstead Press, 2013

'*Canberra's Golden Chapter: Our First Fifty Years*', Roger Pegrum, RAIA ACT Chapter Architecture Awards, 2013

'Defying engineers is a first step to liveability', Roger Pegrum, *The Canberra Times*, 22 May 2013

'Civic should be a place where people can mix', Tony Trobe, *The Sydney Morning Herald*, 18 August 2013

'Sydney Building worth restoring', *The Canberra Times*, 20 February 2014

'Bowen Place Crossing', Roger Pegrum, *Architecture Australia*, March/April 2016

A Very Great City One Day, Roger Pegrum, Barrallier Books, Canberra, 2019

Reviews of *A Very Great City One Day*

Catherine Townsend, 'A personal history of Canberra', *The Canberra Times*, 13 July 2019

Alan Roberts, 'A Very Great City One Day', Canberra Historical Journal, September 2019

Selected Writings

The Year of 45

The Canberra Times

January 1977

Anyone who says that architecture is not a slave to fashion doesn't know an ionic column from a dentil course. Architectural fashions change rather less frequently than trends in skirt lengths and they are certainly harder to predict. Right now there is a dominating fashion in buildings about angles and one angle in particular, perhaps the most neglected angle of all — 45 degrees.

Nowhere is the rebirth of this symbol more apparent than in Canberra. In older and more settled communities 45 must struggle against years of inertia and indifference. In such suffocating conditions it has little chance of usurping healthy idioms like right angles, curves and ziggurats. But Canberra offers no such built history and, being somewhat short on inspiration of its own, is now succouring this enfant terrible. It helps, of course, that architects can have pocket calculators set at root 2 to calculate the length or height of anything.

There were some early indications that 45 was coming. Forty years ago someone timidly cut the corners off Manuka's pleasant corner stores and the arcaded Sydney and Melbourne Buildings in Civic. But now the use of 45 is not limited to plan layouts and can be found in elevations as well. In rare cases it takes control of horizontal and vertical planes simultaneously.

45 is now found in residential architecture and in institutional buildings such as the excellent Churchill House by the late Robin Boyd. Ecclesiastical possibilities have not been ignored and the new Seventh Day Adventist Church in Turner has 45 in two directions at once. A close cousin to the church is the new CSIRO library at Black Mountain where it is suspended above the ground instead of slipping into the water.

In a city based on equilateral triangles (but which has only two buildings of that shape) it is unusual to find 45 triumphing over 60. The future for 60 looks bleak. By comparison, 45 has hardly started to walk. In a few years it will break into a healthy trot with the completion of the National Gallery, a consummate use of 45 in every direction at once. This prominent building will no doubt influence the High Court next door and may even affect the new Parliament House.

At the north end of the central axis, Mount Ainslie has been crowned with a 45 degree viewing platform. The possibilities on Capital Hill are endless and the use of 45 within a square at the apex of an equilateral 60 could be a fascinating exercise.

Not even the new towns will escape the power of the new angle. Belconnen will have the biggest use of 45 on plan in a large and ungainly government office project. Woden will escape only because it is too square, although the medium density housing at Swinger Hill has made a strong bid for the diagonal. Tuggeranong remains virginal so far but it is confidently predicted that she too will yield in time.

There is however a cloud on the horizon with rumours of a new cult that worships the circle. For many years, of course, the circle was spurned because it was considered too difficult to draw and too costly to build.

The big question in the architectural world is when will the curve come? Preparing for the new fashion will require careful planning if one is not to miss the boat. After all, no architect wants to be called old-fashioned.

The Job for a Genius

The Weekend Australian Magazine

August 1977

WANTED: An architect to design Australia's Parliament House. He/she must have 10 years to spare and be prepared to defend the design against all-comers. In return, payment will be a small fortune in fees, fame, prestige and, probably, a knighthood (or whatever else is considered a good gong in 1988). Applicants must be Australian, in good health and with a proven track record in designing large and complex buildings, etc etc

This invitation will never appear in any Australian newspaper, but something very much like it will soon be issued to Australia's 5000-odd architects. At last our biggest, most expensive and most important public building is about to get out of the ground (or into it). And the person who will design it is likely to become the most debated, applauded and vilified architect of our short history.

The whole exercise promises to be very exciting. No one who has been into Canberra's Parliament building can deny it fails to provide quite the same feeling as you get walking through Westminster or the United States Capitol.

Those who work there are noticeably outspoken about its shortcomings, although not only that accounts for our representatives' indecent haste to escape from Fairbairn airport every

weekend. A new and appropriate building will please the members and staff, impress the visitors, and make a fortune for the manufacturers of photographic materials. It may also be seen as a sign of our growth to national maturity—but that's something we should, perhaps, leave for the historians to decide.

Unfortunately, it is doubtful whether Australians as a whole are very interested in architecture. We see Canberra as a neat and tidy Federal city boasting fine roads, a clean lake, and a whole lot of nice white buildings. Most of the bigger buildings are covered by the blanket term architecture, but not all of them are actually good examples of what architecture can be. Guaranteed public interest in the new Parliament House will stem principally from the fact that it is going to be the permanent Parliament House—not that it may have any particular degree of architectural merit.

Nevertheless, some architect will have to design it and control its construction and commissioning. Who will get the job? Will it be a good building or even a great building? Just how does one determine who is going to be immortalised as the creator of Australia's most important single building?

The first and most obvious reaction to

this dilemma is to have a competition. How else can Parliament select the building which will be its home into the 21st century? The English did this when the old Palace of Westminster caught fire in 1834. They got a marvellous building in exchange, one which gracefully exudes a tradition far in excess of that due to its age.

Closer to home, the new Australia used a competition to find Walter Burley Griffin and his elegantly simple town plan for Canberra. The National War Memorial, the symbol of our indebtedness to those who fought in World War I, was the result of a competition in the 1920s. Then there was the competition for the Sydney Opera House—horribly tardy and expensive, but arguably the only real piece of architecture in Australia.

The list of competitions goes on—what about the Carillon in Canberra, the gift of the British Government but the result of a competition among British and Australian architects? The designers of the National Gallery and, most recently, the High Court were determined in the same way. Overseas the same answer is given, whether it is to build a new city hall for Toronto or a squatter re-housing settlement in Manila.

For a long time and in a great number of societies, it has been accepted that the best way to select an architect is to

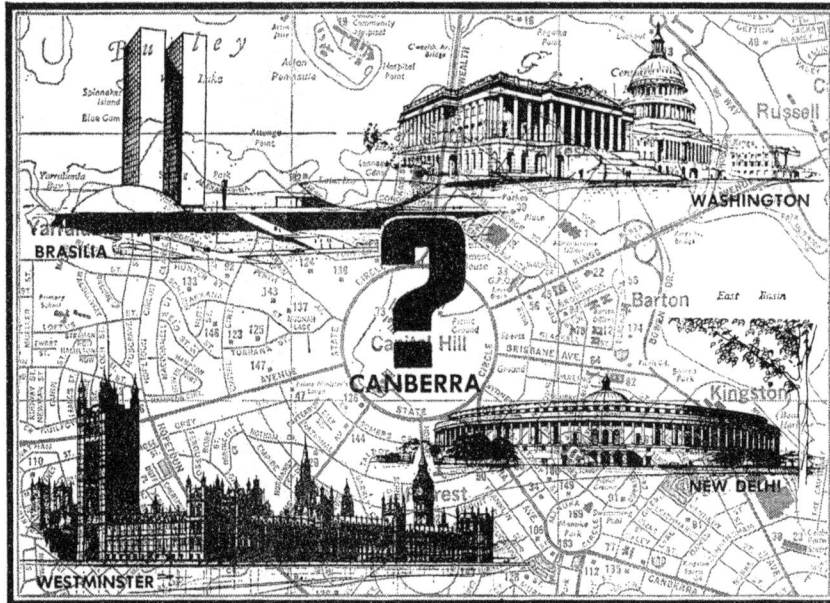

invite design solutions. From the entries, often running into many hundreds, there has usually emerged a singular solution and its creator becomes the person who gets the job.

In what other ways can an architect be chosen on merit? Well, you can always do your research and make up your own mind who is most likely to come up with the goods. That way you lay yourself open to making a mistake but, if your homework is thorough, all should be well—and at least you save the not inconsiderable cost of running a competition.

It's all very confusing, particularly as we can't very well limit ourselves to architects who have designed a parliament house recently. Of course, we could do it the New Zealand way. They by-passed all their own architects and got England's Sir Basil Spence to do the job for them. Whatever system we play for our Parliament House, it is certain some large number of architects and others will disagree with it.

All this would have been behind us if Griffin had succeeded in gaining approval for a competition when he was Federal Capital Director of Design and Construction. The dilemma today must be seen in the light of our parliamentary history, beginning with the interstate rivalries which allowed Melbourne to concede a Federal territory to the larger New South Wales, and take as compensation the privilege to house

the Commonwealth Parliament until it was ready to move to its own home. In the fever of Federation, no one thought that would take very long.

The then Premier of New South Wales, Sir John See, confidently told his State it would all be resolved within five years of Federation. A more astute politician gave long odds that 1920 would not see the Federal Parliament in its own territory—and he, of course, made a lot of money.

The Victorian parliament enthusiastically gave up its large and impressive building for the Federal members, moving itself to the Exhibition Buildings. There they suffered from the cold and complained constantly about the corrugated iron roof—afflictions which Edmund Barton told them should make them feel for 90 per cent of Australia's citizens. Melbourne was an elegant town and no one joined a stampede to leave it behind and move to a bush capital.

It was 1927 before the reluctant politicians took the steamer or the train to the vagaries of Canberra's climate and liquor-less hotels and hostels.

By 1950, it was time to drag Canberra into some sort of modernity. A Senate Select Committee in 1955 recommended that the planning and construction of Canberra should be entrusted to a statutory authority, something like the corporations then developing new towns in England.

By 1957 this had led to the creation of the National Capital Development Commission and high on the list of things for the commission to do was to locate those buildings not yet constructed.

Griffin's plan was subtly altered by the Commission—instead of a railway station on Mt Pleasant we got a defence Pentagon; in place of some of Griffin's departmental buildings we got a National Library; and the arms of the triangle became Kings Avenue, Commonwealth Avenue and Parkes Way (the last instead of the more logical Constitution Avenue).

Yet no one touched Griffin's site for the Parliament House, which, for 50 years, had been Camp Hill, a low rise directly behind the 'provisional' Parliament House. Nor did anyone really know what to do with Capital Hill, the apex of the parliamentary triangle. It was here that Griffin saw the People's House, a large and flexible arena for public oration and ceremony—all concepts rather popular at the turn of the century but somewhat embarrassingly chauvinistic in the 1960s.

It soon was apparent that planning of the central areas could not proceed until agreement had been reached on who would do what where.

In 1965, Sir Robert Menzies arranged the formation of a Joint Select Committee to inquire into and report upon the accommodation needs of the Senate, the House of Representatives, staff, visitors, and the press. It was March 1970, before the committee completed its deliberations and published its findings, now known as the Blue Book.

In the interim, committee members had visited parliament buildings in Kuala Lumpur, New Delhi, Rome, Bonn, Washington and Ottawa. Their report showed the complexity of the problem and made valuable spatial and circulation recommendations. But they were not asked to design the building and, wisely, they refrained from doing so.

Things slowed for a while after that but judgment day had to come. By 1974, the NCDC noted planning must soon commence in earnest, for the existing building was 'spatially inadequate, functionally inefficient and mechanically obsolete'. It was decided that Parliament should now choose its final resting place. A strong lobby for Capital Hill had developed and, after heated propaganda from all sides, Capital Hill was chosen in place of Griffin's site on Camp Hill.

The Select Committee had done its work and in August 1975 was replaced by a more permanent standing committee of both Houses. Its joint chairmen are the President of the Senate, Senator Condor Laucke, and the Speaker of the House of Representatives, Billy Snedden. Its 12 members include the Minister for the Capital Territory, Tony Staley, and the Speaker in the Whitlam Parliament, Gordon Scholes.

The resolution appointing this powerful Committee gives it the role as the 'client for the new and permanent Parliament House in all matters concerned with the planning, design and construction'.

The immensity of the task, outlined in the Blue Book, has been reinforced by the work of the Standing Committee. The Committee's first report was issued on May 9 this year, the golden jubilee of the present building. Working now in association with the NCDC, the Committee recommended it construct on Capital Hill a building with an ultimate floor area of almost a million square feet—8 hectares, or 20 good-size football fields. On 1977 figures, the cost for the first stage of about 4ha will be about $128 million.

Whatever happens during the next 10 years, some factors will be constant, and some of these should be isolated from the mechanics of building. One factor has already been mentioned—the complexity of the planning problem. But then there is the vexing question of the client—a variable group of politicians and an equally disparate array of governmental and public users whose needs may—and probably will—clash frequently.

First, although the physical planning is complicated at all levels, there is by now a firm Westminster-style parliamentary system. In 1901, there was an unmanageable political triangle—the Protectionists from Victoria, the Freetraders of New South

Wales and the then Labour group made government difficult. In due course this settled down to a two-party system, and in the new Parliament this will require a similar duplication of the present facilities.

Then there is the Senate—75 years old and quite likely to pass on or suffer radical change. In 1897, William Morris Hughes (then a Labour man) spoke out vehemently against the idea of a States' House—'that the Senate was to be elected made no difference', he said, 'as none but the rich man, boomed by the press, could ever hope to canvass such enormous electorates'. If an Upper House is to live on, it will require its own chamber and facilities, much as now, and all comparatively simple as a planning exercise.

The confusion in planning does not then centre on the main parliamentary offices or debating chambers, but in the way in which these activities cross with those of non-members—the public, the distinguished guests, the public participants in the committee processes (where so much of Parliament's work is done), the library—and its incredibly important systems for information storage and retrieval—and, of course, the press.

It was these sorts of conflicts of interest and precedence which made the High Court competition difficult. It is one thing to physically isolate all discrete activities and introduce endless check points at cross-overs, and another thing altogether to guide the user unobtrusively along his or her appropriate path.

Just as justice should be seen to be done, so must Parliament be seen to ease the transition from elector to elected, and vice versa.

The architect must recognise this situation and the building must reflect democratic processes. Away must go all the hard edges of space—the public should not feel locked out from the system of government and the politicians should not feel themselves either isolated or imprisoned.

To this dilemma must be added the most difficult factor of all—responsiveness to change. The Parliament is not likely to be threatened by physical assault,

yet the Canadian Parliament, sitting in 1850 at Montreal, was attacked and its buildings set on fire by the dissident British colonists.

How do you make a 'soft-edge' building defensible? At Campbell Park, the newest Defence Department building in Canberra, this was done by lifting the entire building six metres off the ground. That solution will not work on Capital Hill.

Then there is the omnipresence of the media representative. Will the proceedings of Parliament be televised regularly? Can this be done without large numbers of OB vans and antennae and without streams of cabling run through open windows? Will the committees require television coverage from time to time? Can all this be built into the fabric of the building?

And so it goes on, without doubt the most challenging invitation to combine ceremony with security, technological convenience with spiritual enjoyment in a miniature city with a resident population of a few thousand and a floating cast of a million extras a year.

First and foremost, it must work properly, but it must also represent the national ethos. Like the making of a cake, not only must it have the right ingredients well mixed and well baked, it should also be exquisitely presented and finely decorated.

Who will be the cook?

Currently the NCDC thinks it will be an Australian architect, and few people would deny we now have a body of architectural skills which obviate our need to run overseas for help. But the Commission does not think the architect should be chosen by competition, and its final advice in this regard will have great weight with the Standing Committee and, ultimately, with Parliament.

Competitions, the NCDC believes, are most appropriate when the design problem is either familiar or relatively simple, so that good solutions are normally found for housing, office buildings, monuments and less-involved public buildings.

But for Parliament House, the NCDC says, Australia should look first for a designer, then for a design. In this way, the chosen architect will be able to work through the morass of planning requirements in close association with the client, solving the contradictions more competently than would be possible if asked to do the same thing in competition and in isolation from user response and guidance.

The NCDC intends to choose the architect from all those who nominate themselves. Each architect will be required to set out his or her record of achievements (in some way not yet determined). From the responses, likely to number 100 or more, selection will be made through a weeding-out process that will take several months and involve interviews and, possibly, some further graphic presentation (but not, it seems, an actual competition for the design of this particular building).

On the timetable of the Standing Committee, the architect will be nominated early in 1979. The design/construct program will then be started in the normal way.

The alternative is a competition for a design, not a designer. For years the Royal Australian Institute of Architects has maintained a policy of commissioning major public buildings by a two-stage open competition—the first stage seeking ideas, the second stage involving greater detail by about half a dozen selected entrants.

West Germany has more than 40 competitions every year, and it is true to say these architects are suckers for competitions. In a profession where

you are not allowed to advertise, the chance of instant fame is too good to pass up.

Roger Johnson, head of the School of Environmental Design in Canberra, feels competitions are marvellous things 'to get young people going' and he is currently involved with his students in a competition for a library in Iran.

Because competitions have been used so much, and because the subjects have often been important buildings, it is easier to point to the problems than to the successes. The Opera House in Sydney has become a modern-day albatross which will require some shifting.

A lot of competitions end in nothing being built—the elegantly simple building selected in 1972 as the winning design for the Westminster Parliamentary Building was abandoned in 1975, ostensibly on the grounds of cost but really because none of the politicians wanted to run the risk of being moved into the new building and away from what they saw as the centre of power in the old Barry building.

Yet competitions produce more great buildings than disappointments and, in the present era of strong architectural expression, manage to ensure the widest canvass of ideas. In effect, what the NCDC now intends is still a competition, but one based on track record rather than potential. Despite the democratic appearance of its proposal, the NCDC will surely see that a well-known person will be chosen, and all the young hopefuls will realise this.

It will be a hard-fought battle between the big names of Australian architecture, and the winner will probably come from the left end of the establishment. It will be a war worth watching, with a prize of the kind which usually comes only once in the life of a nation.

If the people of Australia involve themselves, the battle may yet take a different turn. What Australia must get in the end is the very best building, and our stature will be measured by that, not by the name of its designer.

There is still reason to question the methods of the NCDC without impugning the motives and, indeed, a competition may well produce the same person who would emerge from the proposed evaluation procedures. But then, it may not—and the risk of getting a bad design from a good designer is a large one, even for a nation of gamblers.

The Fenceless Society

The Weekend Australian

November 1977

Fewer Australians each year can afford to build their own home. Even if they are able to arrange for the floor plan and internal space to suit them, there is little hope that the street will be visually harmonious or provide a safe area for children. In the move from small communities to large cities, we give up to others the right to determine how our home environment will pan out.

Although most of us can recognise the lack of community in suburbia, not many of us are prepared to take the necessary steps to ensure that what we get is what we really want. To do that, you have to co-operate with your future neighbours.

Co-operative housing is new to Australia but not new to the world. It assumes that housing is a verb as well as a noun, and that real and measurable benefits are possible from consulting each other and pooling ideas. Co-operative housing is part of the platform of both our political parties. The Liberals would probably call it free enterprise in action. Labor might call it socialism in action. Either way, it may prove to be the salvation of our cities.

Most experiments in public participation and community planning have been horrible disasters, but in Canberra there are now two co-operative housing developments that might signal the advent of a real alternative to the standard quarter-acre syndrome.

It is appropriate that the Federal Territory should foster such a return to self-determination. One of the major criticisms of Canberra's suburbs has been the lack of innovation in housing design and siting and the lack of a real understanding of the sort of living community that makes sense in these confused times.

Behind the two Canberra schemes, one in the Tuggeranong valley and one in Belconnen, is Sydney architect Michael Dysart. Dysart's early interest in the role of housing in the creation of a community brought him design awards for a range of project houses. But because the siting of a project house comes after decisions by others on road alignments and land subdivision, he found little opportunity to integrate the house into a cohesive plan for the community. Privacy and a sense of belonging or of place are usually impossible in piecemeal planning. These can be built in only if the twin streams of house design and siting can develop together.

One-third of all housing in Sweden and Switzerland is built as a response to the wishes of common-interest groups. In 1973, the National Capital Development Commission released several sites for co-operative housing schemes. The first group of Canberra citizens to embrace the idea was offered a four-hectare site at Kambah, overlooking a reservation for a golf course. About 150 Canberrans created the Urambi Co-operative Housing Society, taking its name from

a low pair of hills near the area.

Despite its name, the Society was made up from a number of smaller groups, each with their own ideas of the philosophy and form that their community should adopt. Dysart was engaged as both architect and planner. Hopefully, he would be the catalyst to bring their diverse dreams to fruition.

The 150 interested members of the Urambi Society expressed their aims clearly: 'to create a sense of community by providing a grouping of dwelling units which encourages human interaction, to maintain individual privacy and make the communal aspect far more positive than current suburban and medium-density solutions'. The Urambi members accepted Dysart's planning proposals and supported his design objectives. It was not so with the later community group in the Belconnen suburb of Cook.

Dysart recalls that four major sub-groups emerged at Cook. 'There were the elderly, whose sense of traditional community was high. There were the socially innovative, quickly labelled as the trendies, whose ideas centred on introverted, tightly knit developments, where people lived in each other's pockets. There was a strong group of professional pragmatic people, concerned with getting on with the job, and there was an evangelical group who wanted 'a little church on the hill'. It would be Dysart's job to satisfy the needs and wants of each of these factions.

'It was shattering,' he said. 'I walked away from those meetings feeling as if I had been to an intense encounter group ... it was just as shattering for the members. The people who came through at the end were those who had no strong affiliation with any self-interest group ... those who wanted it to work for a wide range of people and lifestyles'.

It was enormously time-consuming to extract decisions and get a consensus of opinion, but the results at both Urambi and Cook would seem to justify the effort. Early agreement was reached to banish the car to the outskirts of the area. Those who felt the need to have their cars near their house have moved in close to the garage spaces. 'If you bring the car inside', says Dysart, 'you end up designing around the turning circle of a garbage truck'.

The economic advantages are real. Construction of community facilities and landscaping adds to the basic construction costs of each house, but the quality of the houses, their increased floor areas and the share of swimming pool, tennis courts and so on provide a high level of amenity at a competitive price. Moreover, every owner has the house he or she wants, chosen from 16 building types, but sited where they wanted it and modified and customised with a kit of extras and accessories.

There are other less tangible benefits. 'Intrinsic to the idea is a better sense of community. People are involved with decisions and can see the results of their efforts. Gone is the immediate alienation a person feels when they move into a conventional private or public development. The whole point of the exercise is to allow self-determination.'

Co-operation is an integral part of both design and lifestyle, but Urambi is not run as a retreat from reality. Each house has a strata unit title and each owner has a say in the operation of the village. And people will sell and move on, all exactly as they might in a development planned for them, not by them.

Apart from using similar external materials, the developments at Kambah and Cook are quite different in form. Urambi threads its way along a single extended pedestrian mall. The larger Cook development climbs dramatically up the wooded base of a hill, presenting a romantic outline reminiscent of a citadel town.

It has been suggested that a possible danger of residential developments at this scale is that in the process of removing alienation from within, a sense of aloofness from the rest of the suburb may result. Starting with Swinger Hill (which was named after a surveyor, and not as a commune for wife-or husband-swapping), Canberra has acquired a number of modern 'prestige' zones in a supposedly egalitarian city. Will these co-operative housing groups acquire an unwarranted snob value?

Michael Dysart recognises the risk but claims that this is only the first stage in the life of a community and that time will tell. The community structure is strong, he says, and would not be threatened by a greater degree of physical integration with standard housing around it. 'The really important thing', he says, 'is that people, not government agencies, are doing this and that our society allows this to happen'.

In an overall mix of subdivisions for detached housing, town-houses and home units, there ought to be a place for people to say what they really want and pull together to make sure that they get it. That is people power at its simplest, and the first developer to recognise its potential will make a bloody bomb.

Urambivillage.com

Towards a New Tower of Babel

Quadrant

March 1979

In this shrinking world, it is difficult not to be aware of the difficulties that are caused by the lack of a single means of communication. Over the past hundred years, there have been a number of attempts to create a universal language – one that, in theory anyway, would always allow us to understand what everyone else is saying. Some people have seen in this challenge something like the search for a universal religion; others are more realistic and would settle for the adoption of one of the existing languages in a simplified form. It is a challenge that has attracted idealists, reformers and a good number of cranks. While children absorb themselves with pig-Latin and Chelsea, grown men and women have spent years creating and polishing languages that might one day unite mankind.

It is a daunting task. There are at least fifteen hundred different languages already in use in the world, and some experts put the number as high as ten thousand. It seems that the last thing we need is yet another language, even if it were possible for this new language to bridge the vast gaps between our thousands of tongues. The pragmatists say we should instead choose one of our major languages – perhaps English, which has half a billion users, or Russian, which has two hundred million, or French or Spanish.

The universal adoption of any one existing language, suddenly or gently over time, would be very difficult to organise. Every nation that lost its language would be indignant, to say the least. For this reason there has been only one significant attempt to solve the problem in this way – so-called *Basic* English, a system created in 1932. All the rest of the effort has gone into creating a synthetic language that would be easily learned by people with a range of mother tongues. In the process, some unusual languages have emerged.

The first modern artificial language was published in 1880, by Johann Martin Schleyer, a German priest. Called *Volapük* (meaning 'world language') Schleyer's invention enjoyed a dramatic but brief popularity. Schleyer claimed at the time that anyone could learn his language within a few weeks, a claim that was really quite ridiculous. It seems that Schleyer spoke fifty languages, and that he assumed the rest of the world shared his ability with words, which they certainly did not. Nevertheless, by 1889 there were three hundred *Volapük* societies and twenty-five periodicals devoted to the language. Within the next few years the bubble burst, and *Volapük* is now no more than an historical oddity.

The faults of *Volapük* were to pop up in many later synthetic languages. Its grammar was absurdly complex. When spoken, the stress had to be always on the second-last syllable, which rendered it useless for most poetry, although the same rule made it ideal for regular blank verse. When written, *Volapük* had all the characteristics of a made-up language. There were nineteen consonants and eight vowels – the English a, e, i, o, u, plus the German ä, ő, ű. The numerals from one to ten were *Bal, Tel, Kil, Fol, Lul, Mäl, Vel, Jől, Zű, Bals,* hardly a logical collection. All names of things were masculine (feminism not then being around) and the feminine form of a thing was created by adding *of* to the male form – *blod* was 'brother', and 'sister' became *of-blod*. Thus 'ten sisters' was *Bals of-blod*. Its verbs were tortuous and gave no promise of being easily grasped by anyone. 'I write' became *penob*, which seems harmless enough, but 'let me write' translated as *penob- őd* and 'I should write' became *äpenob-őr*. From a priest, it might also have been expected that a better translation of the Lord's Prayer could have been arrived at than *O Fat obas, kel binol in sűls, paisaludomőz nem ola* ...

The immediate if brief success of *Volapük* showed that there was a body of people at the end of the nineteenth century who were ready to embrace a universal language. The next language to arrive was *Esperanto*, the only artificial language that still survives to any extent.

Esperanto (meaning 'he who hopes') was the creation of a Polish doctor, Ludovic Zamenhof, who published his Esperanto under a pseudonym in 1887 when the popularity of Volapük was at its peak. Originally presented in Polish, Esperanto was quickly translated into Russian and (rather badly) into English. By 1889, there were two magazines publishing in Esperanto and a German/Esperanto dictionary had appeared. Four years later, Charles Dickens' short novel The Battle of Life appeared in an Esperanto translation, by which time there were already thirty-three books on Esperanto in twelve languages.

The overwhelming initial acceptance of Esperanto reached a peak before the Great War, when it might have been said to be an ideological bridge between the restless nations of Europe and East Asia. When Zamenhof visited the United States in 1910, the Washington Evening Star broke with tradition by publishing its headlines in Esperanto.

Zamenhof and his followers believed fervently that Esperanto would unite the races of the world but, when he died in 1917, Zamenhof had had little financial or spiritual reward from his years of work with Esperanto. H.G. Wells wrote at the time of his death that Zamenhof was 'one of the greatest specimens of international idealism'. Leo Tolstoy became an early supporter of the aims of Esperanto, as did many other men of letters. Today much of that fiery enthusiasm is gone, although it is thought that about a hundred thousand people still speak Esperanto, mainly in Europe and Japan. More than thirty thousand books have been published in Esperanto in its ninety-year history, and in some countries the language is taught at secondary school levels. The great dream of acceptance by the United Nations is however still a dream.

The vocabulary of Esperanto is drawn from root-words common in the majority of six major languages – English, French, German, Italian, Spanish and Portuguese. Such words, once accepted into Esperanto, do not change except for minor adjustments in spelling. The alphabet has twenty-four consonants and five vowels, but these are inflected rather awkwardly. One of Zamenhof's early translations was of Shakespeare's Hamlet, the soliloquy from which shows the typical style of written Esperanto–

Cu esti dŭ ne esti,—tiel staras
Nun la demands: ĉu pli noble estas
Elporti ĉiujn batojn, ĉiujn sagojn
De la kolera sorto, aŭ sin armi ...

Like Volapük, Esperanto requires a strong emphasis on the last syllable but one, and Hamlet's words therefore follow, more or less, the original spoken stresses. It is impossible to alter the meaning of Esperanto by punctuation, however, as meaning in English can be, something for which children learning the new language might be grateful. The problems with Esperanto arose, not from its complex appearance, nor from its accents or the derivation of its vocabulary, but from its unusually simple rules of grammar. Esperantists divided early into those who sought to 'enrich' it by subtle variation, and those who defended the basic faith. As the number of rootwords rose from the original nine hundred to more than six thousand, it was inevitable that it would spawn a rebel cult.

In 1907, a French Esperantist, Louis de Beaufront, published (anonymously at first) a new Esperanto, which he called Ido, meaning 'off-spring'. De Beaufront is said to have been working on his own language, called Adjuvanto, which he had abandoned when Zamenhof published Esperanto. The ranks of Esperantists split for a while but remained faithful eventually to the original and the life of Ido was only fractionally longer than that of Volapük.

The first lines of the Lord's Prayer in Esperanto and in Ido show the slight constructional differences between the two–

Esperanto
Patro nia, kiu estas en las cielo sanktu estu via nomo

Ido
Patro nia, qua esas en las cielo, tuo nomo santigesez

The Idoists objected mainly to the unsuitability of Esperanto for scientific use but also criticised its lack of vocabulary, a deficiency solved in Esperanto by vortfarado (word manufacture). De Beaufront gave the Esperanto translation of 'a rotary transformer might be called a motor generator' as turnighan alispecigilon povas nomi motorproduktanto, which means literally 'a self-turning otherwise-making instrument can be called a motor producer'.

In 1922 Edgar de Wahl launched into the world Occidental, a further variation of Esperanto. Another ex-Esperantist, the Danish linguist Otto Jesperson, waited until 1928 to present his new language, called Novial. But by then the turn-of-century romance with artificial languages was over and neither Occidental nor Novial gained more than a small following.

A somewhat better result had been obtained in 1903 by an Italian mathematician, Professor Giuseppe Peano, who christened his brainchild Interlingua. The sub-title to the language, Latin without inflections, gives the clue to the basis of Interlingua, which adopts all the words common to the Esperanto roots, but includes also Russian root-forms, and all Anglo-Latin stems. It was the proud boast of Peano's Academia pro Interlingua that any word in Interlingua could be found in a school Latin dictionary.

There is no doubt that Interlingua was easier to read than any other synthetic languages around at that time. The English alphabet was adopted without change and plurals always ended in s, so that for an English-speaker at least there was something familiar about the written version. But like all made-up languages, Interlingua looks a lot of the time like a schoolboy code, and with its predominance of French and Italian word forms reads rather like a romantic version of Katzenjammer German.

The cause of Interlingua was resurrected in the 1950s, mainly in the United States, but was not helped by the compilation of a useless dictionary (siderographia = siderography; fricasee = fricassee) and by a tortured mass of prose examples such as per rumper le osso on protera forsan rectifier su gamba (we might be able to strengthen the leg if we break the bone), and *si ille attende langa, ille habera un barba* (if he waits long enough he will have a beard).

The lure of a universal language attracted another mathematician in Lancelot Hogben, better known as the author of *Mathematics for the Million*. Hogben's effort, called *Interglossa*, was written while he was an air-raid warden during the Second World War and was published by Penguin in 1943. The language contained exactly eight hundred and eighty words, no more, no less, and each was numbered. These words, which Hogben called 'vocables' were sometimes more recognisable to an English-speaker than their *Esperanto* equivalents – the prepositions in particular. 'Around' (*cirkaŭ* in *Esperanto*) became *peri*; 'before' (of time) (*antaŭ*) became *pre*; and 'instead of' (*anstataŭ*) translated as *vice*. However, *Interglossa* set a trend in arbitrary words, too. 'Mouse' was *micro muri*; 'rat' was *mega muri*. But Hogben assured his readers that they would find his language simple to master, with the encouragement that

Czech or Chinese
Learn it with ease
Basque or Bantu
Can too.

Since the War, each new artificial language that has emerged has shown an obsession with brevity of form at the expense of convolution of grammar.

Picto and *Arion-Boera* were practically still-born, as was the 'neutral universal language' called *Suma*, published in 1966 by a New York physician, Dr Russell. *Suma* had two thousand basic words, all very short and with alternating consonants and vowels. Russell must have had a distaste for complicated medical terms, for he managed to translate just about all of them into his four-letter newspeak. The word 'vein' becomes *vusu*, so that 'phlebitis' is *vila vusu somo*, and the femoral artery is *fito kasa tobo vusu* (literally: long red blood tube). *Suma* had five vowels and only fourteen consonants, and Russell told the world that each nation could pronounce it as they wished – which sounds like a real recipe for disaster. The childish word construction inevitably leads to some amusing translations. 'Thou shalt not commit adultery' is rendered in *Suma* as *ne davi biki*, which sounds more like a commandment to take your fingers out of the cookie jar.

Yet another 'universal auxiliary language' was published in 1962 by a seventy-year-old Japanese philosopher, Fuishiki Okamoto, who claimed that the language he called *Babm* 'could be used freely by the natives in the Himalayas and the islanders of African ravines'. There is no evidence that either group has yet heard of *Babm*, and it is a safe bet that they would find it quite useless. Whereas Dr Russell's *Suma* reads like a lexicon of medical terminology, *Babm* concentrates with an ingenuous zeal on the higher planes of philosophy and bodily purity.

As in Suma, most words in Babm have only four letters, and these would need to be carefully pronounced and often written down if the meaning is to remain clear. A reader used to English word forms must be particularly careful. In *Babm*, *rgin* means 'kiss', and *rgan* means 'living in sin'; *rojn* means 'pressing cheeks together', while *rjon* refers explicitly to sexual intercourse. *Cop* is 'superior', *copg* (which is a bit difficult to say anyway) is 'magnificent', but *copp* translates as 'comic'. The clergy suffers a similar fate to that of the police, for a 'teacher of religion' is a *pezt*. *Sexs* means 'to repay a loan'; *bnop mopfo* is *Babm* for 'a dog scampers'. Any hopes for the possibility of a flowing prose style disappear when the author explains that the *Babm* translation for 'the span of our bodily life cannot exceed a hundred years' is *Kbom ed kopbagb deb cei bod cop pe dlob*. Try saying it.

Esperanto aside, artificial languages seem to have run their extraordinary course. There remains the chance of a renaissance of a 'dead' language, as Hebrew was revived for the Jewish people and Latin for the Catholics. Neither of these languages is simple, nor is it possible for much of the world to use existing speech habits with them. If these criteria are to be met, there seems little chance that any existing language, living or dead, will become universally accepted. English is the most commonly used language on earth, yet it is a major offender by its complexity. At the end of the last century, the biggest dictionaries of English contained about a hundred and twenty thousand words but a modern comprehensive dictionary lists more than four hundred thousand words. Much of this staggering increase comes from the proliferating terminology of science, but not all.

The chief attempt to simplify English – both in vocabulary and in syntax – has been *Basic* English (an acronym for British, American, Scientific, International, Commercial), a universal language proposed by Charles Ogden in 1932. Ogden claimed that it was possible to write and speak perfectly good English by using no more than eight hundred and fifty words and by following a few simple rules of grammar. Three hundred of the three hundred and fifty most common words in the Bible make the list; the ten most common words in Modern English (the, of, and, to, a, in, that, is, I) are there and the total vocabulary is broken down into groups of words – the names of six hundred 'things' (Ogden eschews the use of the word 'noun'); a hundred and fifty qualities (i.e. adjectives); fifteen acts (verbs); twenty directions (to, from, up and down) and a few dozen sundry extras.

Ogden was claiming firstly that English had as much right to universality as any other living language, and secondly that English could be used in a more simple way than it had been. As to the needless proliferation of words he has ample evidence. Professor Jesperson (the man who dreamed up *Novial*) supported studies which showed that peasants in the 1930s had a vocabulary of twenty-six thousand words, about six thousand more than Shakespeare. There seemed to Ogden no reason for any person to know more words than were necessary for Shakespeare, and after some fundamental research he decided that in fact no one needed more than the *Basic* eight hundred and fifty.

The thought of being restricted to a mere eight hundred and fifty *Basic* words is probably threatening to most people, and the knowledge that one's entire vocabulary can be typed on a single foolscap page would not help things much. But for someone learning English, the conciseness would be a great advantage. Ogden noted that there were fewer words in *Basic* than there were members of the English Parliament, and that an average student whose mother tongue was not too far removed from English would learn all the words in thirty hours.

The use of the *Basic* words and no other would also relieve the burden of learning to spell too many words. There have of course been many attempted reforms of our spelling system. More than a century ago, Jacob Grimm wrote that 'were it not for a whimsical, antiquated orthography (spelling), the universality of English would be still more evident'. Indeed, a revised system for written English had been published as *World English* in 1888, only one year after the appearance of *Esperanto*. This World English discarded the letters c, q, and x, keeping the rest but adding a number of vowel inflections and a weird collection of new symbols for the stranger sounds of spoken English. In the following example, *ꝗ* means th, v is pronounced *ƒ*, ꞁ is an r used after a vowel, and *ꞑ* is the sound we know as ng. With these clues, the meaning might be clear even if the appearance is a little odd -

ꝗ Idē'a ov yùnivèꞁ sal laꞑgwij has ôlwāz bin a fasināti ꞑ wun.

Ogden's *Basic* eight hundred and fifty words allow a more recognisable communication between people, although it is often necessary to use rather stilted expressions in the process. For scientific or other specialist uses, Ogden forsaw an additional hundred and fifty words as all that would be required for any particular area. But for a book on housing in 1934, Raymond McGrath needed only thirteen such extra words to describe architecture. The *Basic* Bible, on which work began in 1930, uses a hundred extra words for reading verse and fifty special words (altar, blessing, kingdom, saint, sin etc.).

Basic English received support and use from many quarters but has not yet received the endorsement it sought to take over as the universal tongue. Perhaps one day it will prevail, for its aims of simplicity make it a more likely contender than any of the artificial languages. Some nations have tried to simplify their own language in the same way – in 1931 Brazil, the largest Portuguese speaking country in the world, adopted a recommendation for a revised official language, but failed to see it through. Meanwhile the fifteen thousand Cree Indians of Canada say *kisāpowatukinumoowepesim*, where we would say January.

In the beginning, says Genesis, 'the whole earth was of one language and of one speech'. But the gods were not keen on the Tower at Shinar rising to meet them in the heavens so they went down to 'confound their language, that they may not understand one another's speech'. The Tower-building stopped, and the people wandered off over the world talking in strange tongues (and incidentally, the building industry was never the same again). Genesis says that the Tower was called Babel 'because there the Lord confused the language of all the earth'. The abuse of language seems to have begun with the writing of the first Book of the Bible, for *Babel* means Gate of God and *Balel* means to confuse. As we live each day with more than a thousand languages keeping us apart, it seems that God has a lot to answer for

A Frozen Moment in a Short History

POL

February-March 1981

We have always been able to learn a lot about past civilisations by looking at the things that they built. Architecture and art have for thousands of years been physical expressions of intellect and creativity and of the way that society sees itself at any particular time. Future archaeologists will certainly have as much fun looking at our society as we have had unravelling the work of our lower-technology ancestors. Of course, we need not wait for that judgment. We can find out here and now what our buildings are saying about what we are.

Not all of our architecture reveals the true spirit of our society. A lot of it is built by accountants, bureaucrats or entrepreneurs for expediency or profit. This is the sort of building that reflects sectional needs and wants. Some of it is elevating and crafted with pride, but most of it is eminently forgettable, temporal monuments to Mammon that will be replaced over and over with movements in fashion and interest rates. Of greater significance in the time scale of history are those pieces of design which have as clients the whole of society and whose value is as much symbolic as it is practical.

Such architecture reflects directly the skills of its creators —the architects, the artists and the artisans —and places on them the heavy responsibility of translating ethos into something we can see and touch. When that happens we have public architecture.

It may be a war memorial or a town hall, a church or an art gallery, and it may express the aspirations of a small local community or of a whole nation. Whatever the scale, in public architecture the symbol is more important than the fabric and its worth is not to be measured by conventional costs and benefits but by its success or failure at solidifying metaphysical needs.

By these standards, the new building in Canberra for the High Court of Australia is true blue public architecture. It is the final solution of an 80-year-old constitutional requirement for a 'Federal Supreme Court to be called the High Court of Australia', in which shall be vested 'the judicial power of the Commonwealth'. It is irrelevant that the members of the High Court may be as few as three, or that they presently number only seven, for the home is what matters, not the residents for the time being. It is equally unimportant whether the building works very well as a courthouse, because one of the features of public architecture is that its detail workings are part of the accepted mystery of the symbol. Like all good public architecture, this new building stands taller than us, safe and reassuring by its size. Clad in the virgin white of priesthood, it represents something essentially non-representational—the omnipotence of the law and the protection that it gives to the structure of our society.

Public architecture does not have to be familiar to be successful. Gone thank goodness are the days when the neo-Goths fought the neo-Greeks for the right to dress the new Palace of Westminster in borrowed finery. Indeed, the opposite is true, for the dreams of today's society should surely be sent forth in today's best clothes. More than 50 years ago, and against most professional opinion then, the English architect and scholar W R Lethaby wrote that 'architecture is a living, progressive, structural art, always readjusting itself to changing conditions of time and place. If it is true, it must be forever new'. Australia's new High Court is exactly this, an up-to-the-minute statement of where we are, a frozen moment in a short history.

It is appropriate that Australia's newest building should be almost completely Australian in design, construction and finishes. It is reassuring and not at all over-nationalistic to know that we did not have to go running off to another country for help in laying it out or holding it up.

This is not to pretend that the new High Court is solely the product of one narrow stream of architectural thought. The building has its roots in a modern international school that has freed world design from smothering stylistic conventions, but it borrows too from the calculated asymmetry of earlier civilisations and is based on a romantic view of space that is as old as theatre. There can be no question about the magnificence of the new High Court symbol and its decoration, but there are still questions to be answered about the distance that has been created between what it stands for and those for whom it stands.

The first impression of the High Court is that it is very high indeed. The main public entrance is at the end of a ceremonial ramp and paved forecourt, and the slow climb emphasises the height of the building in the background. Down one side of the ramp a quiet stream of clear water trickles over a studded bed of grey granite. Designed by Robert Woodward, the rippling watercourse quietly renounces the accepted Canberra notion that water in public places should be squirted as high as possible into the air.

Over the main south face of the building is hung a vast wall of glass. At the base, revolving doors solve the problem of entry in Canberra's severe climate conditions and also keep out the famous blowflies. The other walls of the building are even higher because of the artificial banks that surround them. Behind the east wall is most of the office accommodation. This is not the most attractive face of all—the grey aluminium panels and greenish glass combine with deadly effect. On the west wall things are different again. This is where the courtrooms jut out of the main envelope, giving a broken façade which comes alive with the afternoon sun, in marked contrast to the uncluttered entrance side. The north wall is a carefully moulded composition of large glass and concrete panels. This is an important wall. It faces the Lake and has the job of communicating the symbol over the water. It is also the elevation that balances the National Library in the long view from Mt Ainslie and will culminate in the Parliament House on Capital Hill.

Most of the walls inside and out are in whitish concrete. Sand, cement and gravel for these were stockpiled on the site to ensure a consistent finish through the building. Internally this restraint has helped the public areas which could so easily have become fussy, and the simple concrete

surface is an excellent backdrop for the colourful murals of Jan Senbergs. On the floor are large tiles of Italian marble, which the guide will tell you proudly is the only non-Australian material you can find in the place.

Over the public space is a deeply-coffered concrete ceiling held up by two round pillars 24 metres high. It is truly a building of light and air, responding quickly to the passing of the sun behind a cloud and revelling in the wide open spaces around it and the vistas it frames. It has been called Australian, but more than anything else it is Canberran, acknowledging its setting as no other building there has managed to do.

Photo: Shutterstock

After the splendour of the public hall it is a bit of a let-down to peep into the courtrooms, which look as if they were designed by one or more committees. The ceremonial court has a little bit of everything, three different Australian timbers, some concrete areas and a lot of slotted panelling. Number 2 court is a little better and has the benefit of a long window, so that you can look at Black Mountain if the proceedings get slow. The little number 3 court is certainly the only one where it looks as if the architect beat the building committee. With a glass ceiling through which can be seen the towering main roof, and with simple plaster walls, it is a trifle claustrophobic but that is refreshing

after the ostentation of its bigger brothers. A nice familiar touch in all three courts are the judges' chairs, the same as those provided for the brains on the spot in Mastermind.

Apart from going to the sound-insulated loos (which are under the ceremonial courtroom) or having a drink in the coffee shop with the panorama of the lake before you, that is the end of the places the ordinary tourist may inspect. Way up above are the private chambers of the judges, and their library, common rooms, sitting rooms and dining rooms. As might be expected, these spaces are elegantly furnished and decorated.

The Chief Justice has a spacious suite of rooms in the north-west corner, with a little slit window looking back to the Parliament. The rooms for the other six judges are really rather modest, panelled in timbers of their choice and finely French polished. Their private domain finishes with a small roof garden, where splendid isolation combines with splendid views.

This then is the final repository of Australian justice. Canberra does not have many worthy buildings to represent the national spirit and, even if it did, the High Court building would stand out as one of the finest in concept and execution. A world-class edifice, it nevertheless has not had a flawless past.

Conditions were prepared in July 1972 for a national architectural competition. The tradition of open competitions in Australia is a long one, and some very fine buildings have resulted, but resistance had grown to single-stage competitions which sometimes select an architect and design on rather flimsy drawings and inadequate estimates of costs.

It was decided therefore to use a system new to Australia. The competition would be open to all architects registered in the States and Territories and would be conducted in two stages. Entry to stage one was by registration and the payment of a $25 fee for the design brief and maps of the area. Drawings and photographs of a model were to be delivered to Canberra by December 1972. At least six designs would be then chosen to enter a second stage of more detailed development. The assessors were to include the Chief Justice of the High Court, Sir Garfield Barwick; Sir John Overall, the former head of the National Capital Development Commission; and Daryl Jackson, the Melbourne architect who had prepared an earlier study for the NCDC on the workings of the Court.

From the 158 entries in the first stage of the competition, six were chosen which 'impressed the assessors as being competent designs capable of being developed to satisfy the requirements of the brief'. The selected architects, two each from Melbourne and Sydney, one from Adelaide and one from Perth, were paid $5000 apiece and invited to submit further plans.

It is interesting to see how the six finalists shared remarkably similar ideas on the form of the proposed building, and how closely some of them approached the model suggested by Jackson. In the salad days of the early seventies, architecture on a civic scale had congealed into a bag of tricks that no leading architect could be seen without. Carefully controlled dissonance, floating walls of glass and structural legerdemain were the orders of the day throughout the land and few would dare to challenge that these were essential ingredients for this important competition. By one of those rationalisations that pop up from

time to time in the creative arts, no one saw any inconsistency in subscribing on the one hand to honest expression of function and services and on the other hand to structural dishonesty that allowed masses of concrete to soar impossible distances overhead. Architecture will return to sanity, said one writer at the time, when each floor of a building sits safely on top of the one below.

One of the six final schemes showed promise of being honest and humble and a bit of fun as well. The design submitted by Christopher Kringas, a member of the Sydney practice of Edwards, Madigan, Torzillo and Briggs, was refreshingly simple. The main functional elements were broken up into clearly visible parts, then reassembled with the three courtrooms contained within the arms of the office areas. The major ceremonial court was near the lake but looked back up the slope to the Parliament whose laws it would be evaluating and applying.

Another court was balanced on one leg, so as not to obstruct the direct visual contact between the Parliament and the justices. The third and smallest court was hidden away between the others, but also was lifted above the public hall. Large areas of glass walls and roofs tied the composition together and achieved a lightness that was exciting and by no means irreverent to the symbol. The Kringas design had the additional merit of looking as if it would absorb no more than the stated competition budget of $7.1 million.

In October 1973, Prime Minister Gough Whitlam announced that the design of Edwards, Madigan, Torzillo and Briggs had been declared the winner of the competition. But when the winning design, still with Kringas in charge, was exhibited a drastic change had come over the building. The courts had been pulled back half-way into the main building and a floor and roof garden had been added over the whole composition. Certainly it had become more unified but it had also become monumental. Just as certainly, it no longer looked as if it could be built for $7 million, despite the architect's estimate of $7,124,832.

Ten days before the close of the High Court competition, Sydney's Opera House had ended 15 years of hope and frustration with a gala presentation of War and Peace. Hurried into construction for purely political reasons, the Opera House had been plagued from the start by lack of proper information and performance detail. Estimates of cost had become a standing joke and a State lottery had been started to finance a project that cost $90 million more than it was supposed to. Not that the people of Sydney were unhappy with the building; their complaint was most properly with those who could conceive such splendour with such massive disregard for cost.

Back in Canberra, the lessons of the Opera House had no immediate impact. The winning architects were commissioned to document and supervise the construction of the High Court building. Kringas visited national courts in nine other countries, including the unfinished Supreme Court of Japan, also the result of a competition. By the middle of 1974, sketch plans had been developed further and the architects estimated the cost of the building at $10.5 million. A further $2 million was allocated for the forecourt.

Work meanwhile had started next door on the National Gallery by the same architects. There was pressure from various sources to get on with the High Court—the official explanation being that 'the Whitlam government indicated its desire to commence construction at the earliest possible time'. Only the main structural carcass of the building had been adequately documented in the first twelve months. Details of the large window surfaces were not ready, nor had there been sufficient investigation of the needs of the building for electrical, mechanical or hydraulic services or its internal finishes and furniture. Warning bells from Bennelong Point should have been ringing loud and clear across Canberra.

Using the plans as they stood in July 1974, the National Capital Development Commission and the architects prepared a provisional set of contract documents in October.

When tenders for construction were invited at the end of that month, the official estimate of cost had mysteriously risen to more than $16 million. After negotiations with the lowest tenderer, a contract was let in April 1975, for $18.4 million. This was for a High Court which only two years earlier had been expected to cost the country just over $7 million.

Construction began in May 1975 and Gough Whitlam laid the foundation stone in September. The building program called for completion in 1981, but this was brought forward at the wish of the Chief Justice so that the building could be used for an international conference of appellate magistrates proposed for early 1980. In the event, this was a red herring. The building turned out to be unsuitable for this purpose. As Canberra had no other suitable venue, the conference was held in Sydney and the world's jurists were jetted to Canberra for the day to watch the building being opened by the Queen.

Much has been made of the way that the costs continued to rise over the five years of construction. Even freed from hyperbole, there is something very wrong about a system that allows the public to think one thing when the opposite is actually the case. Half of the contract cost was for items about which little was known. As more detail on the workings of the Court became available and as the refinement of a complex building design progressed it could only be expected that the sums allowed in the contract would prove insufficient. In the end, another $14.8 million was needed to cover work insufficiently detailed before building started and a further $15.8 million was paid out to cover increases in labour and material costs.

The most obvious of the cost increases are related to the windows, the fundamental surrounds of the light and air that made this such an exciting building idea. The Jackson report prepared for the National Capital Development Commission made veiled references to large areas of glass, and noted too that the Chief Justice had no objection to windows in the ceremonial courtroom so that people could look out. No special thought seems to have been given to any problems of security or sound transmission through the windows, although the winning design had double-glazing to control heat loss and gain and special louvres to cut out direct sunlight.

In early 1975, the National Capital Development Commission obtained independent advice on the expected acoustic performance of the various parts of the building. In addition, the Australian Security Intelligence Organisation studied the security aspects of the design. Both sound and security are critical factors in a place for the peaceful evaluation of the rights of society by our leading lawyers. The acoustic consultant found that double glazing could not give acceptable sound reduction in the courtrooms. ASIO recommended that bullet-proof glass should be installed in those windows of Courts 1 and 2 that gave anyone outside the building a direct line of sight to the judges at the bench.

To satisfy the high degree of sound-proofing recommended in the courtrooms it was necessary to change from double-glazing to triple-glazing. This level of control had not previously been used in public buildings in Australia, and is similar to that in Washington's Kennedy Centre, which is on the flight path of National Airport. Triple-glazing has its own problems—temperature build up during the summer can blow out the glass—and to prevent this the heavy glazing units have been connected to a separate air-conditioning system. This required modification to the structure and great care in installation of the glass. To satisfy the requirements of ASIO, one of the three layers of glass was made bullet-proof. Over an inch thick, it is said that eight rounds from an Armalite rifle hitting the same spot will not penetrate it.

Some of the cost of this modification, not expected when construction started, was offset by using single glass in the large walls of the Public Hall instead of the double-glazing originally intended. But this change meant that there would be unacceptable condensation on the inside face of the glass, so fine heated de-misting cables have been run back and forth behind the glass, adding to the cost again. Cleaning an acre of windows has caused problems and extra cost, too. It is fair to say that almost all of these difficulties could have been overcome more economically if the architects had been properly briefed in the beginning and then given the time to resolve them before the building work was started.

The completed High Court is far and away the most impressive building in the Parliamentary Triangle. Nothing can be done to rectify the financial management of its erection, but Canberra now has its own example of what can happen when everyone gets carried away with a good idea. It is important for our society to be assured that the same thing will not happen with the new Parliament House, even accepting that national buildings have a value other than the simple cost of putting them in place.

Chris Kringas died in 1975, and he saw only the very beginnings of his building. Since then the High Court has been the work of Col Madigan, whose previous projects had included the widely-acclaimed Civic Centre for Sydney's Warringah Shire Council. He was also one of the five architects chosen to compete in the final stage of the competition for Parliament House. Madigan holds a belief in what he calls 'inclusive' or 'participating' architecture, which reveals its function and purpose in a very free manner. He shares with Griffin a strong love of reinforced concrete, a twentieth century material with almost limitless potential for spatial form. In his report of July 1973 for the second stage of the High Court competition, Madigan wrote that 'participating architecture makes space its best asset and gives priority to this event over and above what may be considered the conservative luxury of fine finishes'.

More than anything else, it is the spaces of the High Court that inspire the visitor and lead him to understand the symbol. The major spaces are linked by ramps and high walls to give a feeling of continuity rare in public buildings. Perhaps the volumes are too complicated, and few people would be able to reconstruct the workings after one visit. Because of this, the initial reaction is of wonder more than warmth, a result not really antipathetic to the larger aims of public architecture through the ages. Unlike the simple and understandable form of the nearby National Library, the High Court does not fare well in the Mother Test (it's a good building if your mother likes it) and there is a definite inverse relationship between the age of the viewing eye and the degree of acceptance of the building.

Indeed the great danger of public architecture is in building for other architects or for the delight of a small section of the community educated to recognise high values in artistic endeavour. On the other hand, if the principal value of public architecture is symbolic, it is contradictory for it to try to explain the symbol. The paradox had been resolved here with great skill, producing a work that can be admired by artists and architects and at the same time appreciated by the tourist, even if he or she feels somewhat in awe of it all. After all, the law is a bit like that, and neither lawyers nor architects are renowned for their humility.

Hierophants and Apostates
and other Architects

Quadrant

October 1982

a review of
From Bauhaus to Our House
Tom Wolfe

There is, it may surprise you to hear, room in architecture for wit. There is room too for other skills and qualities which may collectively enrich the empirical worth of a building and increase its perceived social significance. That most of our modern architecture lacks humanism and is, by all simple tests, emotionally dead, says a good deal about the education of architects, and something about the society that so mutely pays for it. It may also, if you accept the theories propounded by Tom Wolfe in his latest book, *From Bauhaus to Our House*, show that the blame for our current barrenness came in a dead straight line from the misplaced theories of a small band of middle-Europeans practising a tortured conceit on a gullible Germany fifty years ago.

It all began, says Wolfe, with the Bauhaus, a collective of ideologically-aligned artists and architects founded in the old German capital of Weimar in 1919. The Bauhaus worked within a rigid frame of pedantic political aesthetics. It was headed by Walter Gropius, an aristocratic architect and returned soldier; Paul Klee called him with some reverence 'the Silver Prince'. Moholy-Nagy was there, and so was Marcel Breuer. Mies van der Rohe was a leading figure; he is remembered for his throw-away lines like 'less is more' and 'God is in the details'. The short-lived religion called Mazdaznan sprouted there, as did a health-food craze which provided the Bauhaus with a tasteless diet of uncooked vegetables. With Gropius in the vanguard, this Spartan army set out to convert the heathen mob and succeeded spectacularly. Young architects, says Wolfe, 'went to study at Gropius' feet … some didn't get up until decades later'.

Germany had been crushed and humiliated by the Great War. The old order was gone, its place taken by strutting national socialists. The nation had to be re-built from its ruins and the *Bauhausmenschen* were determined to do their bit in creating a culture fit for a new brotherhood of man. The architectural elite settled on the working man as the beneficiary of their own work, or at least that is what they said they were going to do. Providing for the needs of the worker in the second machine age meant, they said, building them plain, unpretentious boxes. All applied decoration, said the Bauhaus, was bourgeois, a pejorative they threw about freely and grandly to describe anything they didn't like. Curtains, indeed all soft furnishings, were bourgeois and therefore out. So were bright colours, pitched roofs and all those fancy trimmings like fireplaces and skirting-boards. The workers found themselves housed in flat-roofed, slab-sided 'machines for living', white inside and out and with lino on the floor. Unshaded light bulbs screwed directly into new low ceilings and radiators (essential and therefore non-bourgeois) stood to attention in long, narrow corridors.

Little gangs of Frenchmen, Dutchmen and Belgians were meanwhile doing the same sort of thing on blitzed sites for their own lower classes. In the name of honesty, they obliterated anything remotely luxurious before the plans left their drawing boards. The shock of the new was encouraged and paid for willingly by politicians, who saw in these buildings a physical expression of their own socialistic philosophies for the future. The poor working man and his family protested at first, of course, but then gave in and moved in because that was the only option they had. It was really nothing less than a transnational conspiracy, giving European workers housing unlike anything they had ever known and unlike anything that they wanted.

Of course, no architect wanted to be called bourgeois by putting his name to something out of the goosestep, so out they came like bloodless sausages, block after block of worker housing, all looking just the same. It was bad enough that this new 'international style' was all over Europe, but the disease was soon to spread. The first foreigners to see it, and hear the cries of the Bauhaus, were young American architects, and they took it all home with them in wonder. The Americans, until then obedient colonials whose favourite art and architecture harked back to the gentle comforts of rural England or Baroque Italy, found themselves giving refugee status to this Teutonic gospel. No matter that they had neither war nor poor to cope with; suddenly they were home to dozens of Bauhaus clones, building the same black and white boxes. But then the Nazis said that Gropius and the Bauhaus were bourgeois and Jewish, and it was time for the Bauhaus to leave Germany for greener pastures. Poor America got the lot—Gropius, Mies van der Rohe, Albers, Breuer, Moholy-Nagy …

Gropius and Breuer went to Harvard. Moholy-Nagy set up the Chicago Institute of Design. Van der Rohe got the best job—Dean of Architecture in Chicago and the commission to build what is now the Illinois Institute of Technology. Hierophantic fervour ran through a depressed architectural profession. The gods from Weimar and Dessau now had government support in the most powerful nation on earth and academic status to boot, so there was no stopping them. The next generation of American architects got their ideas straight from the Gates of Heaven. And so it was, notes Wolfe, that Modern Architecture became an Institution. All architects (well, almost all architects) still hold true to the Bauhaus line of simplistic—the clean machine is King and to be bourgeois is to be Fink.

There were, thank goodness, some architects who marched to a different drummer. Wolfe singles out the idiosyncratic Frank Lloyd Wright as one. By the time the Bauhaus moved to the United States, Wright was already seventy years old. He had ignored them so far and, by God, he was not going to knuckle under at that age. Wright is the most famous American 'modern architect'. His 1936 house known as Fallingwater flies directly in the face of the box-people, a musical crescendo celebrating man, nature and structure. There have been others, says Wolfe, who ignored the call—Buckminster Fuller, of geodesic dome fame, and Bruce Goff, whose organic work aligns with no mechanical theories. But it is a short list, because the pressure to conform was great, and the failure to conform

meant no work. The big names of today owe their fame and fortune to the Bauhaus—in England, Norman Foster Associates, high-tech, thin-skin artists; in Australia Harry Seidler, whiter than white and mannered as all hell, and Yuncken Freeman, whose BHP black box in Melbourne starts and finishes where Mies van der Rohe started and finished. In America (but also in Melbourne with Collins Place and soon to open in Singapore with Raffles Place) is I. M. Pei, whose East Wing of the National Gallery in Washington is a box with no right angles, smooth and sharp at the same time.

So much for the hierophants. Wolfe's apostates are also Big Names in the United States, but their work is not yet well known in Australia. One early form of apostasy is best described as Camp Architecture—by the very process of breaking the rules and doing it boldly enough to let everyone know what you were up to, designs became excessively metaphorical. Andy Warhol's Campbell's soup can was Camp; so, say some, is the Sydney Opera House. But the Great Non-White Hope for architecture, in Wolfe's vision, probably lies with those who are able to work at their business without dictation of any form from the narrow rules that gave birth to modern architecture.

There have been any number of false prophets, says Wolfe. Most of them have at least one thing in common with the Bauhaus men—they build practically nothing themselves. But can they talk! Here is one of the

New York Five, much pitied by Wolfe, an architect who has built only a handful of houses, writing about his own architectural development: '(the) neo-functionalist attitude, with its idealisations of technology, was invested with the same ethical positivism and aesthetic neutrality of the prewar polemic'. Young architects now flock to this master of words, although I wonder how many know what he is talking about. The outsider, says Wolfe, finds him and his cronies utterly incomprehensible. When he goes on to say that his architecture is about 'relationships between relationships', the public has every right to say it is baffled and bored.

It is indeed a pity that Wolfe does not conclude his excellent and absorbing essay with some indication to the poor citizenry that they will one day get architecture that they will like. This is not to say that architects should not be allowed to dream, or experiment, or confound one another with theories about 'syntactical nuances' or 'the semiology of the infrastructure'. But when all is said and done, architecture, even for the workers, must surely be able to have a bit of charm, as well as the core of geometry and politics which it has had ever since Rameses built those pyramids at Gizeh.

Griffin is dead! Long live Griffin!

Architecture Australia

September 1983

I remember the first time I climbed the slopes of Mount Ainslie 30 years ago. Standing at the top, with the strong Australian sun on my back, I was told that I would some day see laid out before me one of the world's great city plans. The view was splendid even then, but I imagine I was rather sceptical about ever seeing Griffin's formal pattern of landscape and buildings imposed on such a vast, dry and quiet countryside. It has taken 70 years to create, but most of Walter Burley Griffin's design is today there for all to see. Those who doubted that it would ever be, and those who did their best to destroy it, are now mostly gone. Canberra, and Griffin's plan, exist as an act of faith.

The elements and broad detail of Griffin's original design are well-known. The plan, wrote Griffin in 1912, was a logical architectural expression of the two major design determinants—the site itself and the function of the future city. The site, said Griffin, could be broken down into a number of natural elements— the distant tree-covered Brindabellas; the three local mountains, Ainslie, Mugga Mugga and Black Mountain; the lesser hills within the Canberra valley; and the flood plain of the Molonglo River bisecting the gently undulating land over the rest of the city site.

The distant ranges, said Griffin, were to be the background 'stage setting'

for the city when viewed from the 'dress circle' on the northern slopes of the valley. The three mountains would be retained in their natural state as the 'termini of as many important vistas as possible', while the smaller hills would one day become the 'elevated foundations for ... buildings of dominating importance'. A dam across the Molonglo River would allow 'triple internal architectural basins' to be wrapped around a central government zone, whose buildings would be reflected in the surface of the water.

Two simple lines across the landscape confirmed Griffin's debt to Renaissance axial geometry and to the McMillan Plan for Washington D.C. Griffin drew a central land axis from the top of Mount Ainslie, down and across the valley floor, over Camp Hill to Kurrajong (now Capital Hill) and on for 30 miles in the direction of Mount Bimberi, the tallest mountain in the federal territory. A secondary water axis from Black Mountain crossed the land axis at the central lake and continued in a south-easterly direction 'to the broad prospect of the Queanbeyan Plains'. The heart of Griffin's composition, the national area, lay on the southern shore of the lake in an 'accessible but still quiet area', contained in a triangle by the lake and two major avenues converging on Capital Hill.

It was, and is, a simple and splendid

concept. In 1955 Peter Harrison said that almost half a century of town planning advances could not improve it. The greatest strength of Griffin's plan, he said, was that it 'did not depend for its realisation on the construction of grand buildings' but on landscape design. 'Buildings are made important', said Harrison, 'not so much by their size, height or architectural magnificence, but by their setting. It is not an architectural composition but a landscape composition'. Edmund Bacon wrote in 1968 of Canberra's 'network of sweeping vistas, vast gulps of fresh air, superbly exciting and dynamic interactions between the peaks of hills and mountains and the movements of people', and went on to say that 'although many buildings, right in scale and location, are downright poor in architectural expression, Canberra is nevertheless a great work of architecture'. Griffin might have been pleased to hear such fulsome praise; two months after his plan had been published it was suggested that he had 'been carefully reading books upon town planning without having much more than theoretical knowledge to go upon'.

The challenge of Canberra and the Griffin plan has always been the vast horizontal scale of the valley, whose enormous vistas defy comparison with the grandest city plans of modern history. 'All that matters in Versailles', it has been said, covers only half

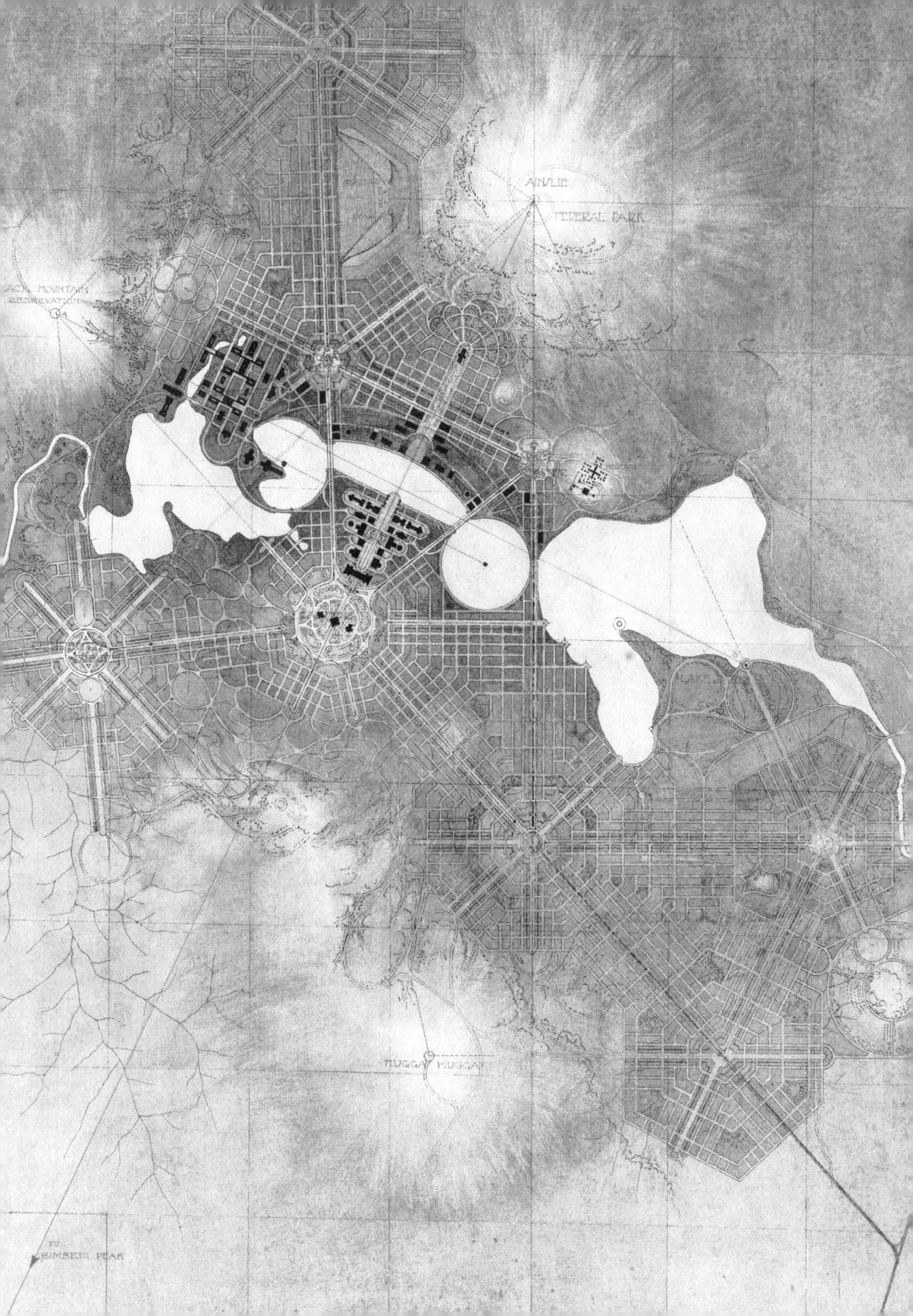

AINLIE

FEDERAL PARK

ACK MOUNTAIN
RESERVATION

LAKE

MUGGA MUGGA

TO
BIMBERI PEAK

the three kilometres from Capital Hill to the slopes of Mt Ainslie. The land axis from the War Memorial to Capital Hill is the same length as that from the U.S. Capitol to the Lincoln memorial, but Canberra's major axis continues on to the conical backdrop of Ainslie. The total composition of Black Mountain, Ainslie, Russell Hill, the lakes and the land south of the lakes is quite beyond the visual comprehension of any ground-level observer, and attention has necessarily been focused on the 450 acres of the central triangle, described by Sir John Overall in 1968 as 'Canberra's great set-piece'. The arguments over the development of this chunk of national real estate have been going on now for more than twenty years and are, I think, far

parliamentary system suggested to him a symmetrical disposition of the two Houses across the land axis. The space between Parliament House and the lake he filled with a formal arrangement of government and public buildings, all defining the land axis within the triangle. His final plans of 1918 gave more detail of a central 'government terrace' halfway between Parliament House and the lake, a 'terrace front' of buildings to complete the lakefront composition, and a watergate to mark the intersection of his land and water axes.

Most efforts to translate this design into a modern reality have been frustrated by the presence of the 'provisional' Parliament House, which is on the land axis but some

parliamentary property and made sure that any axial or broad vistas from within the triangle would be rudely blocked by the considerable bulk of Parliament House.

Whatever the architectural merits of Holford's design, those who understood the broad logic behind the Griffin plan were horrified at what was seen as an attempt to graft a Westminster urban vision onto a very Australian site. Edmund Bacon accused architects in general and Holford in particular of a 'very serious intellectual and perceptual shortcoming ... under which they cannot see space as such, but merely as a void to be filled with structures'. To block the wide views from the national area, he said, 'in complete

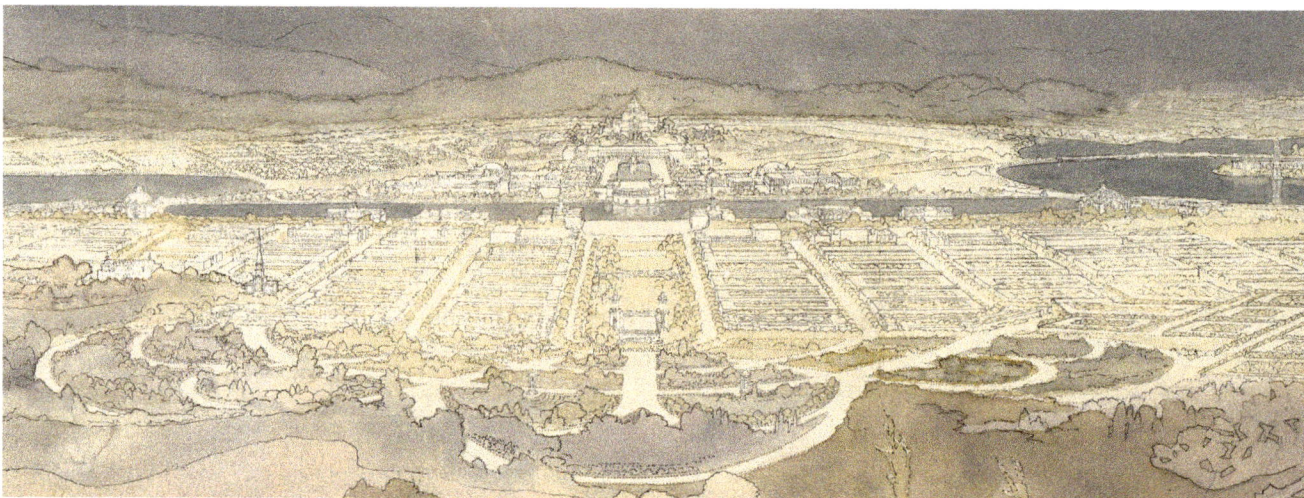

from over. The understandable wish to create an environment worthy of a modern nation and the magnificent site has been complicated by a wavering sense of responsibility to do it all in accordance with the spirit of Griffin's original design.

Since the 1950s there have been many attempts to analyse Griffin's 'design principles' for the national area and to prepare a long-term development plan which would faithfully reflect both Griffin's broad planning aims and his detail symbolism. Griffin's original hierarchical composition was topped on Capital Hill by a 'Capitol' building, 'a general administrative building ... for popular assembly and festivity'. Below, on the spur known as Camp Hill, the bicameral

150 metres north of Griffin's site on Camp Hill. For the ten years after 1957, the considerable difficulties of placing a big new Parliament building behind the romantic little white House were avoided by assuming that a permanent Parliament House would be better placed in the centre of the southern lakeshore. This proposal by the British planner William Holford ignored Griffin's idea of a triangular composition of buildings rising tier on tier from the lake. Holford suggested instead the creation of a 'balanced but not symmetrical development' and a great central space ringed with major office buildings and national institutions. The plan removed Griffin's 'terrace front' of buildings, turned his symbolic watergate into a piece of

Perspective from Mount Ainslie looking south-west towards the background ranges. Griffin described the design of the National Area as '... monumental governmental structures sharply defined, rising tier on tier to the culminating highest forested hill of the Capitol'.

violation of the original concept of the plan, will ruin Canberra as the capital of Australia'. Strong support for Bacon came from Roger Johnson, who argued convincingly that the old Parliament House must be demolished and that there should be a 'great open space in front of Parliament House', the enclosure of which should be formed not by nearby buildings but by Griffin's 'dress circle', the hills north of the lake.

The Holford plan was abandoned in 1968 and new plans concentrated on creating a national 'place' as a foreground for a Parliament House on either Camp Hill or Capital Hill. By this time however the National Library had been built to flank a lakeside Parliament House, a very bland Treasury Building had been put near Commonwealth Avenue to mirror the Administrative Building completed in 1955, and a site had been reserved for a High Court building between the Administrative Building and the lake. On the assumption that Parliament would now be somewhere near the top of the triangle, the High Court was brought nearer the lake and in towards the land axis, from where it could relate distantly but symbolically to the Legislature, and the National Gallery was taken from its allocated site at the foot of Capital Hill and dropped next to the High Court to help balance the lakefront composition. Members of Parliament were said to be happy with the idea of a big front yard and a few scattered buildings on the edges, but many Griffin disciples mourned the losses of a well-defined land axis and a properly expressed terrace of buildings along the lakeshore.

By 1974 all plans were back in the melting pot. In a free vote, the members of Parliament rejected Camp Hill as their future home and decided that they wanted the permanent Houses of Parliament on Capital Hill. Their decision upset those who had pressed the claims of the Griffin site on Camp Hill. The move to Capital Hill destroyed any chance of a national place in front of the Parliament and almost certainly meant that the provisional House would remain floating halfway between Capital Hill and the lake. There was, too, a real fear of a large and overbearing Parliament building towering over the triangle. It was announced that the ultimate floor area of the new building would be about one million square feet. In an age of architectural extroversion, there was a good reason to think that Australia's most important building would end up looking considerably bigger than Griffin's 'objective feature' had ever been.

It was forgotten by many people at this time that Griffin himself had toyed with the idea of a hilltop Parliament House in his original competition submission. 'Were the Parliament in one House', he had said, 'the architectural development ... would differ in only a few details from that of the other one suggested'. As arrangements were being made for a competition for the design of the permanent Parliament House, planners within the National Capital Development Commission sought ways to interpret Griffin's 'architectural development' for the triangle, no easy task with the physical form of the objective feature not yet determined. Things were not helped much by gratuitous advice from foreign observers that 'any building less in scale than the Great Pyramid would hardly read at all' on the top of Capital Hill.

The plan described by Paul Reid (*Architecture Australia*, March 1981) defined five principal elements in the Griffin plan and argued for a development that recognised the importance of these elements. Working from Capital Hill north to the lake, these elements were the objective feature, the brow of Camp Hill, the terrace court, the terrace front and the watergate. The objective feature, once the Capitol building, would now be the permanent Parliament House. The brow of Camp Hill, where Griffin had tied together his composition with a bifurcated Parliament House, still had a role to play, said Reid, as the site for twin buildings framing the view to and from Capital Hill. The Griffin terrace court could still be built as a major punctuation mark on the land axis, and the terrace front of buildings, marking the northern baseline of the triangle, could be similarly completed, albeit in a less formal manner than that indicated by Griffin. The last critical element, a watergate to mark the crossing of the two major planning axes, had been neglected for years. What might have been a mile-long south bank of the lake, drawn by Griffin to parallel his water axis, was no longer there and nor was a symbolic crossing of the axes at its mid-point. The demands of topography and modern hydraulics had splayed the shoreline, and 'the water axis had disappeared into history'. With or without the water axis, the Reid plan urged the reinstatement of the watergate, and the total plan showed that despite the presence of the provisional House, and despite the un-Griffinlike character and disposition of the other buildings in the triangle, it was still possible to re-create much of the spirit of the Griffin design.

The Reid plan was a realistic and imaginative update of the Griffin plan and should perhaps have signalled the end of the wrangling over the future development of the triangle. It discarded the notion of a vast national green park (which in any event was no longer valid with a remote Parliament House) and built instead a hierarchy of varied spaces at a more human scale.

Its building 'jewels' were placed with great care to form both the national symbol and the formal public squares. It was however an 'architectural' solution, certainly not a landscape plan, and it demanded strict control of building envelopes and some subjugation of individual architectural expression for the greater good of the total experience. Roger Johnson had earlier shown his distrust of such an approach, noting that 'buildings do not rise conveniently in pairs'. The symmetry of 'Griffin-derived plans', he said, was unlikely to be achieved within future building programs.

There was of course one great unknown in the Reid plan. Would the design chosen for the Parliament House complete the Griffin painting or would it destroy it? Manning Clark has remarked that the choice of Canberra as the capital site and the selection of the Griffin design were 'two events which have done great credit to humanity'. Such acclaim must now be extended to include those who singled out Romaldo Giurgola's magic answer for Capital Hill. By turning the office windows sideways and building for the hill, not for architectural effect, Giurgola has marked the centre of Canberra's geometry with a non-threatening profile and a lofty transparent symbol. The Giurgola/Thorp solution is, in the words of Peter Muller, 'a stroke of urban design genius'.

The most happy outcome of the Parliament House competition would seem to have vindicated the Reid plan, but in the event it has probably destroyed it. The presence and symmetry of the new House has led inevitably to a renewed emphasis of the land axis, described in the final Giurgola report as 'the fundamental gesture of the city, a line around which all other design has evolved'. The National Capital Development Commission's latest development plan for the national area relies almost entirely on the reinstatement of that axis as the single most important element of the Griffin design. A broad ceremonial avenue or mall now runs from Capital Hill to the War Memorial, broken in its length only by the lake and by the present House. Reid's 'architectural solution' has been replaced by a broad 'shaft of landscaping', and it is now trees, not buildings, that form most of the lines, spaces and punctuation marks of the national area.

On the face of it this is the right thing to do and arguably the only realistic solution. The NCDC plan 'lays down a number of planning and urban design principles and objectives, which in the view of the Commission should be used as a basis for detailed design', and it aims to provide 'an orderly or systematic framework which can serve as a guide for decisions about the locations of buildings, roads and other facilities'. But it is not only a land-use policy document. With its single-minded emphasis of the land axis it is also a physical plan. The NCDC has suggested yet another interpretation of the Griffin design and has opened a further can of civic design worms.

The NCDC plan, with its preoccupation on the idea of a mall, is a clear break from the omni-directional plans of the late 60s and early 70s, when the major assets of an uncluttered national place were seen as 'the sweep of the eye, the relationship of buildings and trees, the distant views, the reflection of water, the absence of noise and the clarity of the light'. On the premise that Griffin's major axis must not only exist but must be seen to exist, the mall is run as a red ribbon through the centre of Canberra, lined each side with the same tall native trees that have graced Anzac Parade for nearly twenty years. It will be a mall on a very

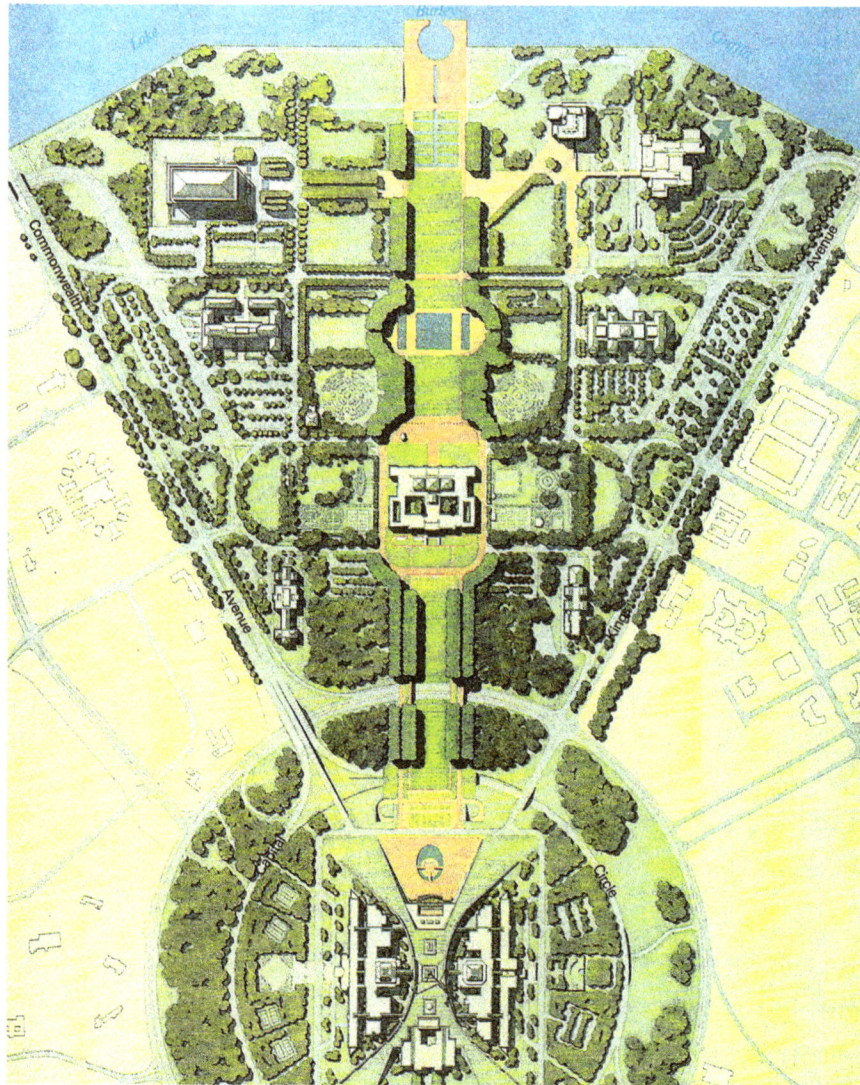

grand scale indeed, during the day brick red edged in grey/green and at night picked out in the darkness by strong white lighting.

By completing the Griffin composition in the long and aerial view as 'a national symbol for all Australians', the plan has responded boldly to the decision to put Parliament on Capital Hill. But it is one thing to achieve broad landscape imagery and another much more difficult thing to create fine urban space on the ground. It is here that the new plan is almost certain to fail. In Griffin's scheme of things, impractical as it may have been, the area between the water and Parliament House was to be a carefully controlled series of spatial experiences, formed by the rising ground, the expansion and contraction of the axial boundaries and the changing surface landscape.

The 1982 Parliamentary Zone Development Plan, prepared by the National Capital Development Commission, showing the proposed mall through the centre of the triangle.

In the NCDC plan no such subtlety exists. Instead there is a mall of 'mercilessly rigorous geometry', deviating fractionally around the existing reflecting pools and punctuated by the 1927 House, but for most of its long length promising little sense of place or space.

The notion of a sense of place is as valid now as it was in earlier civilisations, and the critical factor now, as always, is the human scale. It is expected and hoped that the central area of Australia's capital city will from time to time become the focus of events of national significance.

Such occasions, when related directly to Parliament, will use that building and its forecourt, from which elevated position they may be seen spiritually to embrace the national symbol below. There are however certain to be occasions when pomp and ceremony will more properly relate not to Parliament but to broad national feelings of achievement, rejoicing or regret. Those are the times when the people of Australia will need a place of their own and this latest plan does not give it to them.

This is not to say that the central area of Canberra should be treated as a pedestrian plaza on a super-national scale. Vast crowds may or may not eventuate, but good urban design could create a place where things may happen if they want to happen. The Griffin plan is notable for its lack of definition in this area, and Griffin explained that he had designed for 'the housing of various specialised activities … not for the commerce of the throng'. But the Griffin plan formed places where the mind and the body might wander. It did not drive a monotonous mall through the heart of the city, denying even the most adventurous any hope of excitement and discovery and the more placid any point of rest. Now that our elected representatives have taken for themselves the hill belonging to the people, is it unreasonable to ask that the rest of the area be available for the pleasure of the people, whatever that may turn out to be?

The 'marking of occasions and men' requires that the march of the proposed mall be halted somewhere in its length and somewhere, I suggest, near the middle of things. There is already a minor belling at the reflecting pools, but this is too mean to serve the function. The only other punctuation mark is in front of the provisional Parliament House. Some urban generosity here and a widening of the mall would make an Australian Square without destroying the linear concept of the mall one little bit. Griffin's terrace court will be resurrected, the central area will get a square at a scale appropriate for the island continent, and the Australian people will get their own national place, sheltered from the gaze of the politicians by the comfortable and human scale of the old stucco Parliament. It would indeed be a nice touch if that old building, which has been in the background of every national gathering since 1927, could continue as one wall of a 'place of the people' after 1988.

Hopefully it is not too late to re-think the shape of the proposed mall. At the same time, thought should be given to softening its hard edges, perhaps by the use of trees as a screen, not as a wall. Future buildings along the avenue and around a Parkes Place/Australia Square may then combine with natural elements to form the places Griffin so innocently conceived. It will be many years before such trees and buildings fill the national area and only then will we know if we have done justice to Walter Burley Griffin and to ourselves. In the meantime there is cause for celebration in the reinstatement of the watergate, and in the reinforcement of Griffin's east-west mini-axes. There is still room for manoeuvre over what, if anything, should go each side of the land bridge through Camp Hill, and there is of course still hope for buildings on the northern lakeshore and along Anzac Parade. As those intimately associated with Canberra over the last 25 years would attest, designing and building a modern capital city based on 70 year-old plans is no simple matter. More than anything else, what Walter Burley Griffin deserves now is a sympathetic interpretation of an elusive but wonderful dream.

Give the public what it wants

The Canberra Times

August 2001

a review of
The Look of Architecture'
Witold Rybczynski

When the Chrysler Building was opened in New York in 1931, *The New York Times* sniffed at its stainless steel gargoyles and winged hubcaps and labelled it 'a stunt design'.

Of course, the *Times* got it wrong. The Chrysler Building and others like it are seen today as icons of the Jazz Age, that decade-and-a-bit after the Great War when American society was confident and more than a little brash. In this excellent collection of essays, Witold Rybczynski discusses what makes a building loved or unloved and why some buildings fare better than others over time. He contends that the form and detail of buildings like the Tribune Tower in Chicago and the Bilbao Guggenheim are what architecture is all about. Whether from the recent or distant past, part of the charm of buildings, says Rybczynski, is that 'they reflect old values and bygone virtues and vices'.

Firmness, commodity and delight may well be the three maxims of architecture, but Rybczynski argues that the reason why we keep some buildings and happily put others under the wreckers hammer is because they delight us, rarely or never because they are terribly well built or extremely functional. In other words, we keep interesting buildings which best express the spirit of their times.

The Look of Architecture is based on a recent series of lectures by Rybczynski at the New York Public Library. With wit and numerous examples to support his theories, Rybczynski suggests that, if style is the language of architecture, then it is fashion which represents the wide cultural currents that shape and direct that style.

Fashion, the wish of a society to distinguish itself from the old, may be fleeting, but it is not, says Rybczynski, at all frivolous. Today's architects shudder at the idea of being thought 'stylish' or 'fashionable'. Nonsense, says Rybczynski, they cannot avoid these labels and they should indeed embrace them.

Leslie Wilkinson, the first professor of architecture at the University of Sydney, once said that it was 'not as important to be in style as to have style'. Rybczynski would not have had any of that. Indeed, he is firm in his belief that it is the public, not other architects, whose vote counts as to whether a building is stylish or fashionable and whether it is good or bad. As the mood of society changes, sometimes favouring simple forward-looking clothes and buildings, and at other times wanting richness, colour and ornament, Rybczynski says that architects should give the public what it wants -

An architecture that recognises style—and fashion – would not be an architecture that is introspective and self-referential, as are many contemporary buildings. It would be part of the world

– not architecture for architects, but architecture for the rest of us. And that would not be a bad thing.

There should be more books like this which question perceived reality in a jolly good read. It has been thirty years since the publication of Robin Boyd's *Artificial Australia*, which was based on his radio talks in the ABC Boyer Lecture series. Boyd's book started the search for a modern Australian architecture 'which acts well, speaks well and looks well'. Maybe Rybczynski will be as influential in encouraging architects to build for their society and not just for themselves.

Kenneth Henry Oliphant

Australian Dictionary of Biography

2000

OLIPHANT Kenneth Henry Bell (1894-1975), architect, was born on 10 November 1894 at Bendigo, Victoria, the third son of James Glen Oliphant, a schoolteacher and his wife Hannah, nee Bell. Oliphant's interest in architecture and art was not well received in his family. His determination to succeed as an architect was however clear from an early stage, and his move to Canberra in 1926 provided him with unique opportunities as the first private architect in Australia's new capital city.

After service in France with the 1st Field Company Engineers, Oliphant studied architecture in a Melbourne atelier, where he showed particular skills in residential design. In 1921 he was elected an associate of the Royal Victorian Institute of Architects and commenced practice as an architect. Some of his designs for a two storey house were published in 1922, and in 1925 he published drawings for a parish hall in Kew. Plans and photographs of two of his completed houses in Canberra were published in 1930.

In 1924 or 1925, Oliphant joined the Melbourne architectural office of Oakley and Parkes. This office was formed by Percy Oakley and Stanley Parkes following their first prize submission (with John Scarborough) in a Commonwealth competition for a residential subdivision in Canberra. The competition sought several standard designs for new cottages for senior public servants and parliamentary staff who would move to Canberra with the transfer of the seat of government from Melbourne in 1927.

The Oakley and Parkes designs were for forty residences to be erected in Blandfordia, a suburb to the south of the provisional Parliament House then under construction. Later named after Sir John Forrest, Blandfordia was to be laid out in a romantic and picturesque manner with sweeping avenues of trees, hedgerows and generous private gardens, all of which conformed to the currently popular objectives of the English Garden City movement. The competition area, now known as the Forrest Conservation Area, has been classified by the National Trust and is entered on the Register of the National Estate as a significant example of architecture and landscape planning philosophy in the early years of Australian federation.

Ken Oliphant was not involved in the Canberra competition, but he may have worked in Melbourne on the detail drawings being prepared for construction. There is a clear connection in style and detail between the Canberra designs of Oakley and Parkes and the built work of Oliphant. In 1926 Oliphant was sent by his employers to supervise the construction of the Blandfordia subdivision. His professional association with Oakley and Parkes was apparently a loose one, for he was commissioned later that year for two private residences in his own name, one of these a substantial house in Red Hill for clients who had previously engaged Oakley and Parkes for commercial work in the north and south of the city. Oliphant's almost immediate success as a private practitioner was deserved but not expected. It is reported that Oliphant recognised the risk he was taking when he left Oakley and Parkes the following year, but that he said he would rather starve in Canberra than in Melbourne.

In the years prior to 1930, Oliphant undertook the design of a dozen private residences for professional and business people then settling north and south of the Molonglo River. His designs were varied in style but all shared a simple grace which has in many cases ensured their preservation virtually intact. He borrowed widely from the Georgian and Queen Anne vocabularies, with occasional essays into Tudor, Mediterranean and later Art Deco styles. There was a marked degree of confidence in his siting and building designs and his houses were uniformly finely detailed and soundly constructed. Internally he 'felt the space' and his houses contain fine volumes all beautifully crafted.

Oliphant's palette of external materials included locally made red brick and terracotta roof tiles, with external walls of smooth or rough-cast plaster. These same materials had been adopted by the Commonwealth Architect John Smith Murdoch (q.v.)

Barton Court 1934

in his designs for the first federal buildings in Canberra and were used in many early municipal buildings. A number of churches, hotels and private schools constructed at the time showed similar dedication to the romantic imagery, axiality and garden plantings of Oliphant's houses. This use of a consistent but broad design vocabulary at a range of scales and in all the scattered parts of early Canberra established the delightful character of its original suburbs, and marks Oliphant and other early architects as important figures in the short history of Canberra.

The first rush of government and private building in Canberra was followed by a sharp decline in growth and then by the Great Depression, from which Canberra did not emerge until after the Second World War. In these years, Oliphant designed the impressive Barton Court apartments and was able to maintain his practice

with a lesser number of residential and commercial commissions. He was for many years honorary architect for the Church of St John the Baptist in the central valley of Canberra. St John's was built in the Victorian Gothic style by the Campbell family in 1845 with a splendid tower added by Edmund Blackett in 1884. Oliphant added elegant lychgates in red mahogany, the sandstone altar and later the war memorial shrine.

Oliphant was never at ease with the new styles of architecture which emerged after the War and his later years produced little of the spark which characterised his first period in Canberra. He contributed to the design of the Dairy Farmers building in functional modern style but was more comfortable with traditional forms and materials. He assisted Prof Brian Lewis (q.v.) in the construction of the Vice-Chancellor's residence at the Australian National University and was a foundation

member of the Commonwealth Club in the old Canberra House designed by Murdoch for the first Federal Capital Administrator.

In 1933, Oliphant married Betty Farqhuar, the daughter of a Queanbeyan bank manager. They had two daughters and a son David, who graduated as an architect before entering the Anglican ministry. Ken Oliphant retired from his practice in 1965 and died in Canberra on 10 February 1975. He is remembered as a tall and distinguished looking man who was always well dressed and who could talk to anyone. He believed there was 'an art in everything' and expressed delight equally in the skills of both tradesmen and labourers. His works, which exhibit a firmness, commodity, delight and awareness of place not always found in architecture at any time, together with his community involvement, assure Ken Oliphant a place as one of the leading citizens of Canberra in its first fifty years.

Cuthbert Claude Mortier Whitley

Australian Dictionary of Biography

2002

WHITLEY Cuthbert Claude Mortier (1886-1942), architect and public servant, was born on 30 July 1886 in Rutherglen, Victoria, the first of two sons of Charles Herbert Whitley, a school teacher, and his wife Elizabeth, nee Horrocks. He trained in design and building with the State Public Works Department of Victoria and in 1912 joined the Commonwealth public service as a draughtsman in the Public Works Branch of the Department of Home Affairs. In 1920, Whitley was promoted to the position of architect in the Department of Works and Railways and was admitted as an associate of the Victorian Institute of Architects and the Royal Institute of British Architects.

Whitley became a protege of the first Commonwealth Chief Architect J S Murdoch. Under Murdoch's direction, Whitley prepared preliminary designs for the Commonwealth Bank building in Brisbane and later contributed to the design of the adjacent Commonwealth Offices. At St James' Anglican Church, Camberwell, on 25 January 1913 he married Mabel Tudor with whom he had a daughter and a son.

In 1929, Whitley was transferred with his family to Canberra where he worked under the Principal Designing Architect E H Henderson. During several absences overseas of Henderson, Whitley was Acting Chief Architect, and, following Henderson's suicide in 1939, Whitley was for a short time Acting Commonwealth Architect. At the time of his retirement after a stroke in 1941, Whitley was Senior Architect in the Department of the Interior.

In the decade from 1930, the growth of Canberra was slowed by the Depression, but a number of important public buildings were designed and built in Canberra and Whitley was involved in almost all of these. Under Henderson and Whitley, the restrained colonial elegance of Murdoch's earlier buildings gave way to new building forms with modelled and decorated facades and interiors which reflected their confidence in a bright future for the young capital city and the nation.

Henderson led the way in this with an innovative design for a public swimming pool at Manuka. In 1930 such buildings could not be found outside the state capitals. Henderson set his building at the end of a large public park and decorated his Art Deco entrance with playful shell motifs and wave patterned coloured glass. Whitley's first major project, a new building for the Patent Office on Kings Avenue near Murdoch's provisional Parliament House, was a more serious opus. A formal axial composition with sandstone facings, it is a classical design with restrained Art Deco embellishment, in every respect a bold expression of a modern office building with generous fenestration, efficient internal working areas and delightful detailing.

In 1936, Whitley designed Ainslie Public School, the first primary school north of the Molonglo River. His design is both functional and elegant, with carefully articulated facades and creative treatment of conventional materials internally and externally. Art Deco motifs such as chevrons and vertical flutes reward closer inspection and suggest a more relaxed and forward looking view of education than found in most schools at that time.

Whitley followed this lovely building with a dramatic design for Canberra's first secondary school at Acton. A lofty clock tower marks the high ground overlooking the city centre, with long symmetrical wings of classrooms terminating in bold semicircular ends. The formality of the composition is enlivened with decorative elements beautifully integrated into the overall design. At the time, it was described as 'the most modern school in Australia' and it attracted national and overseas interest. Set in expansive landscaped grounds with large sporting fields, it was a selective school offering a wide range of courses in music, art and languages. The school boasted 'the latest developments in educational practice' with an emphasis on small classes and many technological

innovations including a built-in radio system and provision for the use of slide projectors in all classrooms.

Whitley's ambitions for a truly modern Canberra also found expression in smaller projects. His designs for the city's first fire station in Forrest were a marked departure from the exuberance of his previous works towards a severe functionalist cubism, borrowing heavily from the utilitarianism of contemporary western European architecture, with flat facades and parapets and minimal visual relief. Whitley continued this search for efficiency with a small number of single storey houses north and south of the river. The flat roofs, crisp steel framed windows and unrelieved brick walls of these houses were the first Canberra expression of an Inter-War Functionalist style which became the foundation of all modern architecture in the second half of the twentieth century.

Whitley lived with his family in Canberra in the inner city suburb of Reid, from where he walked each day to work in the city centre. A quiet unassuming man and a Freemason, he had played football in the senior team for Hawthorn in Melbourne and in Canberra won several trophies in golf. He travelled only for work and never went overseas, which is remarkable given his understanding of modern architectural movements in his time. At his death, it was reported that his name would be connected with his fine contribution to architecture in the two schools he designed, to which he had 'enthusiastically devoted his skill and experience for the lasting benefit of the children of the National Capital'.

Robert Charles Given Coulter

Encyclopedia of Australian Architecture

Philip Goad and Julie Willis eds

2011

COULTER, ROBERT CHARLES GIVEN (1864-1956), was born in January 1864 at Parramatta, New South Wales. The youngest of eight children of Irish immigrants, he studied painting and drawing in Sydney with Julian Ashton and became an exhibiting member of the Royal Art Society. He received his architectural training in the Sydney office of John Joseph Davey, where he worked for almost twenty years. In 1900, on the eve of the federation of the Australian colonies, he joined the NSW Public Works Department under Government Architect Walter Liberty Vernon. Among his first projects was the highly decorated pavilion in Centennial Park, the focus of Sydney celebrations at the inauguration of the Commonwealth of Australia on 1 January 1901.

The Australian Constitution required the establishment of a federal capital city and seat of government on a site selected by the Parliament within New South Wales. A congress of architects, engineers and surveyors in Melbourne in May 1901 discussed the form the national capital might take. Coulter presented a colourful painting of a 'waterside federal city' on the shores of Lake George. Coulter's sketch and a similar drawing by Lionel Lindsay of a capital city on the Snowy River at Dalgety focused political and professional attention on the idea of an ornamental lake at the heart of the national capital city.

Vernon encouraged Coulter's talents as an artist and architectural delineator. On the instructions of both state and federal governments, he prepared sketches and watercolour paintings of all the nominated capital city sites and he accompanied politicians on many visits to inspect the various districts. The Canberra valley was selected in 1908 and it was decided to conduct an international competition for the design of the city. Coulter painted two cycloramas that were issued to competitors around the world. The competition was won by Walter Burley Griffin of Chicago, but a design by Coulter with engineer C H Caswell and surveyor W S Griffiths received first place in a minority report by the jury. Coulter's perspective drawings showed monumental buildings each side of a wide waterway, with an arched bridge not unlike the later designs for the Sydney Harbour Bridge.

Coulter produced drawings for many public buildings in Sydney and designed the entrance building, elephant house and refreshment rooms at the new Taronga Zoological Park on Sydney, in which he pioneered the use of ferro-cement construction. He designed exhibits for the Australian pavilion at the British Empire Exhibition at Wembley in 1924 and won first prizes in competitions for a church in Canberra and houses in the garden suburb of Daceyville. He was involved for many years with proposals for the Sydney Harbour Bridge and assisted the chief engineer J J C Bradfield with perspective sketches of the final design. He prepared designs for the granite pylons at each end of the bridge and for numerous light fittings along the carriageways. In recognition of his work on the bridge, Coulter was invited to turn on the lighting system for the first time. It is said that Coulter also designed the commemorative postage stamp issued in March 1932 to mark the official opening of the bridge.

Coulter devoted his life to the care of an invalid sister and never married. He has been described as an 'architect of his time', whose own designs were eclectic and derivative, but whose major contributions to architecture and society are found in his powerful renderings of public buildings designed by others and in his delicate paintings of the landscape of south eastern Australia.

1912 drawing by Coulter of his entry with C H Caswell and W S Griffiths in the Australian Capital Competition

Friends, Lovers, Rivals and Enemies

The Canberra Times

May 2011

a review of
Community: Building Modern Australia
Hannah Lewi and David Nichols eds.
UNSW Press

The federation of the Australian colonies brought with it a fresh look at the roles and responsibilities of individual citizens and of Australian society as a whole. New ideas about social welfare and particularly infant health and childhood education were accompanied by the dislocation of families with growth and change in our towns and cities. This book provides an absorbing account of the hundreds of modest public buildings that popped up in every part of Australia—the libraries, mothercraft centres, pre-schools, swimming pools and other facilities that were felt necessary for healthy living and for the establishment and maintenance of modern twentieth century communities

At the end of the Second World War, the older city neighbourhoods were emptying and any sense of urban community was draining away. An unseemly rush to outer suburbia with its characterless town planning and unfamiliar housing types brought even more pressure to bear on the fragile structure of society. This book reminds us that both individuals and families could see the fabric and workings of this brave new world as alienating and remote. Subtle shifts in the way these concerns were addressed saw the post-war philanthropy of Labor governments re-directed by Menzies and his successors to more individual aspirations and re-directed again by Whitlam's policy makers to include multiculturalism, new social movements and community consultation.

The idea of 'togetherness' as a central component of a 'community' has been steadily diluted during these modern times. More than a century ago, the German sociologist Ferdinand Toennies described the breakdown of traditional community life as a move from *Gemeinschaft* (community) to *Gesellschaft* (association). Quoting Graham Day, the authors of this book argue that whereas the word 'community' suggests 'a lasting and genuine form of living together ... through coordinated action for a common good', the term 'association' implies a rather 'more calculated action on the part of individuals who engage in artificial relations for what they can get from one another'.

Whether or not by the 'calculated action of individuals', the passion to build the full range of community-based facilities had all but burned itself out by about 1980, when the measure of success in such things became efficiency and financial accountability. It didn't hurt either if construction and completion could be timed to suit election cycles. An impressive bigger building was suddenly more attractive to local politicians than small buildings dotted about the town. Far better to lump them all together and give them important names like multifunction community centres or civic centres or worse. But it is the simple little lending libraries and health centres and scout halls and rowing sheds that are remembered by our parents and grandparents with affection and gratitude. It is these places that are recorded in all their ordinariness in this illustrated catalogue of our salad days for community facilities.

Canberra is surely Australia's premier social laboratory, and we got our fair share of appropriately scaled community facilities from the very beginning. In the older parts of Canberra there is a weatherboarded baby health centre across the road from almost every suburban shopping centre. Not far away are playing fields and landscaped parks, small suburban church halls or kindergartens with neatly tended gardens. A Women's and Infants' Health Society was established in Canberra in 1926, before the Parliament had even moved from Melbourne. Until only recently, the Queen Elizabeth II Home for Mothers and Babies operated from what looked like a large country house right in the middle of our grandly named Civic Centre.

We treasure these signs of social interaction and shared community obligations, carefully dropped into place by the early planners. But not

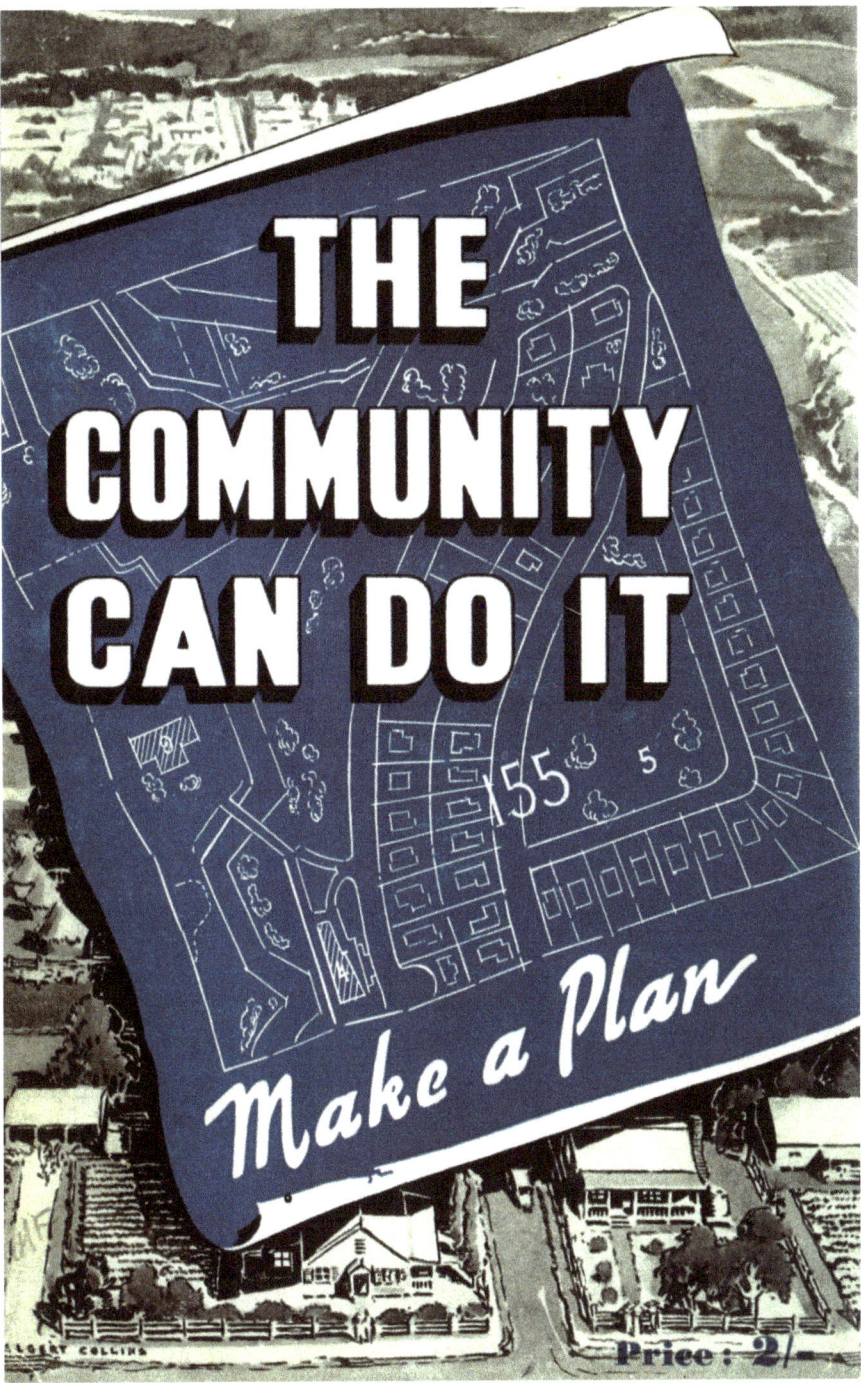

THE COMMUNITY CAN DO IT

Make a Plan

155 5

Price: 2/-

everything in Canberra survives the onslaught of time and money, and the risk of death by indifference hangs over almost all of these smaller public buildings. Enrico Taglietti's lovely library in Dickson has been unnecessarily fiddled with and Harry Seidler's fine bowling club in Griffith will make way very soon for lots of boring flats.

Nugget Coombs spoke in 1942 of the need for the 'proper grouping of homes in communities' and he referred to libraries, social and political clubs and sporting facilities as the 'capital equipment of human relationships'. It is in these places, said Coombs, that we will find our friends, our lovers, our rivals and our enemies and where the 'essential business of life is carried out'. Maybe the essential business of life now takes place inside large shopping malls or in those huge social clubs with poker machines and cheap restaurants, but I hope not. A book about those places would be deadly dull.

101

An Avenue of Distinction

The Canberra Times

May 2012

The construction of Constitution Avenue is a once in a lifetime opportunity to build a wonderful Main Street in our national capital city. When Walter Burley Griffin left Canberra 95 years ago, the line of Constitution Avenue was shown on his plans as 'Capital Terrace'. He described it as the 'municipal avenue' of the city, which brings with it an image of the commercial centre propping up the seat of government on the other side of the lake. This would be the femoral artery of the city, a wide and tree lined boulevard to rival the picture postcard avenues of older cities elsewhere. Regrettably, the current plans for Constitution Avenue will fail to achieve these objectives.

Construction of Constitution Avenue was a major proposition in *The Griffin Legacy,* a review in 2006 of how the dignity, robustness and inherent flexibility of the Griffin plan could be harnessed to complete its unrealised elements. The Legacy was followed by Amendment 60 to the National Capital Plan, which sets out the design objectives for Constitution Avenue. What is required, said the Authority, is an 'elegant, simple and bold design emphasising the geometry and formality of the main avenues'. There will need to be 'appropriately scaled street trees' with 'consistent pavement materials, street furniture and lighting' and it is important to ensure the 'safety and comfort of pedestrians'.

In real estate terms, Constitution Avenue ought to be *the* street in Canberra and its top city address, but the current design is unlikely to deliver this dream. For starters, it is listed on the ACT government website under the topic 'transport'. Further clues as to the design emphasis at play can be found in terms such as 'upgrading the corridor', 'traffic movement' and 'enhanced public transport'. Talk of a long-term vision for Constitution Avenue as 'a vibrant, mixed-use, tree-lined grand boulevard' is diluted with a relentless emphasis on efficient systems for wheeled traffic.

Constitution Avenue is *not a road*, it is a street. As a rule, all roads in towns should be streets. Traffic movement is a paramount concern with roads, but streets do that and more to establish the character of the public domain. Traffic is a central issue for roads and parkways and highways, but Constitution Avenue is none of these, it is a *street*.

In Scotland, the design of streets is 'not principally about creating successful traffic movements, it is about creating successful places'. In any town or city, say the canny Scots, the street will have two key functions —place and movement —but place must come first. Streets can be pleasant and flexible settings for human activity or they can be alien, unattractive and unsafe. In the case of Constitution

Avenue, it would seem that making a successful place for people comes a distant fourth to the movement of buses, cars and bicycles.

Generous and continuous sidewalks are essential components of a safe and attractive city street. Constitution Avenue is 45.72 metres wide, which is about three-quarters the width of Northbourne Avenue. It is proposed to build a public footpath 2.8 metres wide on the north side of Constitution Avenue, hard up against the property line. There is then a narrow 1.1 metre easement for trees and a 2.8 metre space for short runs of kerbside parking, and immediately after that you hit the cars and the buses. This is not the sunny side of the street, so the total 6.7 metres from property line to kerb will always be in shade. Of course, new buildings on this side of the street can be set back but this doesn't make the footpath any more generous unless you also move the front property line. There will not be too many people walking or talking or drinking coffee on the north side of this street.

On the other (sunny) side of the street, it will be about 17 metres from the property line to the kerb, but this is bisected by a 3 metre wide dedicated cycleway between the trees, so the space is not solely for those on foot and is not without risk. The perambulations of the pedestrian are again under threat at the crossing with Coranderrk Street, where slip lanes in all directions at once means that a pedestrian must cross the street via at least two triangular refuges. This continues the existing arrangement, which leaves pedestrians stranded on concrete islands in a fast-moving stream of cars and buses. It also thumbs its nose at the instruction in Amendment 60 for intersections 'designed to minimise slip lanes for fast turning traffic'.

Along Constitution Avenue there are presently up to four rows of oak trees, planted almost fifty years ago. Some are in good condition, some not so good, there are a few ring-ins and many are missing. All have been neglected and are in need of pruning and shaping. Row 1 on the north side of the road is to remain. Rows 2, 3 and 4 are on the other side of the road and are spaced about 7 metres apart All the trees in row 2 will be removed for the length of the avenue, but rows 3 and 4 will remain, with the new cycleway between them. And there will be a whole new row of oaks down the middle of the road in a median strip. Axial lines joining hilltops and low prominences are the basis of Canberra's Beaux Arts planning. With a centre median and trees, nobody looking along Constitution Avenue will ever see Mt Pleasant or City Hill

In order to get some idea of how this might all look on the ground, it is useful to visit Lonsdale Street in Braddon, which has mature plane trees in 6 metre wide verges and a fragmented central median with occasional large deciduous trees. There are two lanes of slow-moving traffic each way with metered kerbside parking and there is also some staggered parking in the centre of the road. The overall width of Lonsdale Street is 30.48 metres, which makes it only two thirds of the width of Constitution Avenue, but the distance between the closest trees at each side of the street is about 22 metres, which is only 2 or 3 metres less than for Constitution Avenue. In the 25 or so metre width between the trees on Constitution Avenue must be fitted 2 bus lanes, 2 car lanes, 2 rows of kerbside parking and a median strip 4.8 metres wide with a tree in the middle. It will be a tight fit.

In response to the invitation for feedback on the proposed design, the following thoughts are offered.

Move the centre line of the street another three or four metres to the south and make the north sidewalk at least ten metres wide. Provide pedestrian crossings at the centre of city blocks as well as at intersections. Delete the central median and its trees; the street is not wide enough for this and it adds nothing to the place. Kerbside parking is shown in blocks as if the trees on each side of the avenue were opposite each other. It may be better to provide a small number of kerbside parking spaces in the gaps between the existing trees. Put the cycle path(s) on the roadway; this is a low speed road and the danger to cyclists is no greater than elsewhere in the city.

Buses and bus stops should be put back on the kerb line with allowances made for future tramlines and tram stops down the centre of the avenue. Tramlines should be straight and not wander from side to side as is shown for the buses. At Coranderrk Street, repeat the simple arrangement of pedestrian crossings shown for Anzac Parade. Paint as few lines on the road as possible. Minimise visual clutter and road signage. Aim for a design that is elegant, simple, bold and timeless.

Thought must also be given to the pattern of future land subdivision along the avenue, including the lengths of frontages, gaps between building blocks and service access. Indicative block layouts and an arrangement for servicing from rear lanes were shown on Griffin's 1912 competition winning plans and on all his subsequent plans. These would be a good starting point when we complete this important Canberra street and give it the quality and urbanity it deserves.

A big, bold, simple concept

Speech at the launch of *A big, bold, simple concept* by Alan Roberts
at the Australian Academy of Science, Canberra

27 April 2010

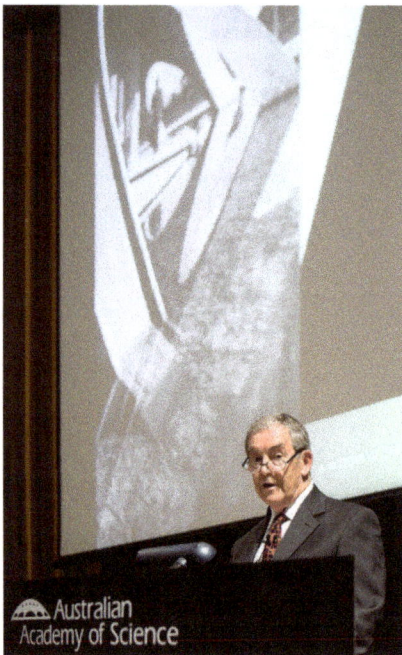

This is a truly wonderful room and we are in a wonderful and very romantic building, a unique product of a scientific age when design and human endeavour seemingly knew no limits. Many Canberra architects are familiar with this hall, because the Academy of Science kindly lends it to the Institute of Architects every year for our Walter Burley Griffin memorial lecture. It would be difficult to find a more appropriate and inspiring venue for an event named for the visionary designer of our capital city.

I may know your building a little better than some of my associates because I have been in Canberra for so long. I watched the dome being built when I was a student at university. That was a time before I really understood what architecture could be, and I certainly did not know then what a great human achievement this building would prove to be. It is therefore a particular pleasure and honour to be here 50 years on to welcome an excellent book about a truly great building and about the ordinary and extraordinary people who brought it into being.

Buildings are central to our lives, our work and our play, but they don't move and they don't speak clearly to the majority of people, and mostly therefore they are taken for granted. It needs a gentle and persistent ear and a sharp eye to unravel the stories built into the form and fabric of any building. Architecture is never an easy thing to write about, even for architects, in fact especially for architects, who are likely to disagree as often as they agree. Alan Roberts has done an excellent job in telling the professional and human stories in the making of this building. He has brought out the fire and the passion of both the scientists and the architects and he skillfully describes the challenge and the fun of making architecture.

As you will all know, this building was the product of an architectural competition, in this case an invited competition among seven Australian architects. Architects are suckers for competitions and have been for centuries. Open and anonymous competitions, in particular, sometimes throw up previously unimagined possibilities, and they are often the only way for young architects to show their mettle in the widest forums. An open competition for the Vietnam Veterans Memorial in Washington DC 30 years ago was won by a 20 year old Chinese American student of landscape architecture. Those who have been there will, I am sure, agree that it is perhaps the most awe-inspiring outdoor space any of us could ever see.

Canberra has a long association with architectural competitions. Walter Burley Griffin was a 35-year old architect in Chicago who had built a few interesting houses but nothing really special. Then, with his wife Marion Mahony, he worked through a long mid-western winter to give us an elegant vision for a capital city of the world's newest democracy, set in a landscape he had never seen. The Australian War Memorial, at one end of Griffin's land axis, and the new Parliament House at the other end were found at different times by competition.

The motives for competitions are of course not always as pure as the winning designs. The Sydney Opera House competition was conducted at almost exactly the same time as the competition for this building. It started life as an election stunt, but we must now be grateful that the NSW government of the day was so worried about its re-election. A United Nations competition in the mid-70s for the design of community housing for squatters in Manila produced an outstanding and sustainable solution, but after a part of it was built Imelda Marcos said it looked like a slum and had it knocked down. Politics and ego can get in the way of just about anything.

But this book and this building show that you can get a great result too from an invited competition. In this category this building shares a place in Canberra's design history with the Carillon on Aspen Island, chosen from a similarly small field of six architects, three Australian and three British. A competition of any kind demands commitment from everyone, most particularly from its sponsors, and that is also what happened here. Professor Mark Oliphant, the first President of the Academy, felt that only a competition would find them 'a first class building ... that would express the spirit of science'. Otto Frankel said the Academy building would be an 'adventure' for them all. 'We were agreed', he said, 'that this must be an outstanding building in every sense'. The Fellows had wisely dismissed running off overseas to a fashionable or predictable name architect like Walter Gropius, or Mies van der Rohe or le Corbusier. It was the Australian Academy of Science, they said, and they would have an Australian architect and that was that.

I digress here for a moment to refer to the birth of the Australian Academy of Science during the busy Royal Visit to Canberra in February 1954. School children from Canberra and all around played our parts at several events that week. We gave the Queen a jolly good cheer at Manuka Oval one morning and later that day sat on a small hill near where the National Library now stands to hold up coloured placards

and make a display of the Australian flag. I was told it was a terrific-looking flag, but maybe that was my mum trying to make me feel good. During this visit the Queen unveiled the Australian-American Memorial at Russell Hill (also the result of a design competition). On Tuesday 16 February 1954 the Duke of Edinburgh opened University House in the morning and that afternoon the Queen met with the council of the brand new Australian Academy of Science at Government House and handed her royal charter to its President. From all reports there was much celebration all around. And so started Frankel's great 'adventure'.

Over the next year or so, the Academy put together a veritable Who's Who of Australian architects and the race was underway. Each of the submitted designs is included in this book, and provides a window into the state of Australian architecture in the post-war boom years of the 1950s. You will have seen the original drawings on display in the Jaeger Room. You will agree, I am sure, that, apart from the winning design by Melbourne architect Roy Grounds, none of the entries took the opportunity to come up with a significant architectural statement which addressed both the splendid site and the expectations of the client. But then you need only one good design from a competition, and the Academy got that in spades.

Those architects invited to submit were at the forefront of their profession. Roy Grounds, the winning architect, and three of the other architects would go on to receive the Gold Medal of the Royal Australian Institute of Architects, its highest honour. There was a design from Kevin Borland and Peter McIntyre, who had designed the Swimming Hall for the Olympic Games just then finished in Melbourne. That building was, and still is, one of the great pieces of modern sporting architecture in Australia. Their proposal for the Academy was not up to this standard. Then there was Fowell, Mansfield and Maclurcan, a young practice from Sydney, whose design style I would describe as 'Whitehall modern', timeless and a bit formal. In Canberra, examples of their work can be seen in the Treasury Building in Parkes and at the

Commonwealth Club in Yarralumla. Their design for the Academy gave it a generous forecourt facing the Institute of Anatomy and was elegantly rendered in pencil.

The design of Adelaide architects Hassell and McConnell was similarly axial, with a generous foyer and an imposing curved facade to the west. The Hassell office went on to design the Festival Centre in Adelaide. I confess to some familiarity with this office because my twin brother Tony, who was also an architect, joined Hassells from Canberra in the early 1970s and became a partner soon after. I had some knowledge also through Tony of the Melbourne-based firm of architects and engineers Mussen MacKay and Potter, who had been involved with the John Curtin School of Medical Research. I also came to know later the only Canberra-based architect in the competition, Bob Warren, who had moved here from Melbourne in the early 1950s. The list of architects for the competition was rounded out by the Melbourne office of Mockridge, Stahle and Mitchell, who submitted a lozenge shaped design to the Academy. In Canberra they later built a number of schools, but they are best known here for their design of the HC Coombs Building, which they won in a limited competition. I understand that within the University their building is known as the 'catacombs' because it is notoriously easy to get lost in and it is said to have 19 different levels and 30 external doors. I have not counted them ...

But it was the mesmerising design of Roy Grounds that got the brave scientists all atwitter. Grounds' work had been described by his partner Robin Boyd as 'modern medieval' and later as 'very old and very new at the same time'. As we discover in this book, the striking drawings of the dome were the first things the members of the Academy selection committee saw when they came into the room. These drawings made then, and still make, an unforgettable impression and the committee was drawn back to them over and over. It must have been like this in Sydney with the Opera House competition at almost the same time, when

Joern Utzon's drawings, suggestive, spidery and incomplete as they were, put all the other proposals into the shade. Grounds had hoped that the building he was offering to the Academy was something that men of science could understand and in due course embrace. What happened instead was that they fell in love with it at first sight and have cherished it ever since.

But settling on an architect and a design concept is only the first part of the building process and Alan Roberts moves on to an exciting account of the trials and tribulations in getting this building into and out of the ground. Roy Grounds was by all accounts a strong minded man, somewhat larger than life in the style of the well-known American architect Frank Lloyd Wright. Gifted people are not always easy to get on with ...

Grounds had some trouble over the next year or so with the fellows of the Academy, who were not always happy with the way he was developing his design. This sort of constructive conflict is not rare, particularly when the client and the architect are both strong-minded. Alan Roberts gives us a ringside seat at their discussions and debates. Grounds was then 50 years old and Oliphant had just turned 55. Each was at the height of his professional life and neither, I imagine, was used to being told what to do or how to do it. Grounds had made his name in Melbourne, where he enjoyed almost total control of design decisions. Oliphant was no shrinking violet either. Towards the end of the Second World War, he had been the man sent to America to tell the Americans to get on and split the atom. Two strong minds meeting, not always in the middle. At one point, we are told in the book, Grounds went to meet the building committee with crayons and large sheets of paper, handing them out and saying that if they were not happy with what he was doing, they could perhaps show him how to do it their way and better.

But the mix of architects and scientists was to be a magical combination of talents and energies. Grounds later described his building as 'a portrait of the scientists as I saw them—full

of mystery, romance and intense intellectual exercise all at the same time'. He said he wanted 'serene simplicity in their meeting room'. That is this room and there is no doubt he got it. He was looking too for what he called a 'sense of enormous disciplined order', which he said 'is the way their minds work', and he wanted 'a big emotional impact because they are very emotional people'. At one point, Grounds said the scientists were 'a group of very mysterious men' (there were no women then). But he also acknowledged the positive impact that the Academy had had on him and his design. 'A few times in my life', he later said, 'I have done better than I can do'. This building was certainly one of those times.

Canberra was a small but lovely town in the 1950s and I have fond memories of our life here. I am grateful for the inclusion by Alan of my father's name among the many people who contributed to Canberra and the making of this building. We came here from England in 1948, and my father added a little over 6 meters in height to the dam on the Cotter River. During the War, he had been a civil engineer with the British Admiralty and he had worked on the temporary harbours known as Mulberry and the undersea supply lines called Pluto. The line of his work on the Cotter Dam is still there but will soon be covered by a huge new earth wall. Such is progress. In the mid 1950s, my father was the Territory's chief structural engineer and one of his jobs was to approve the structural design for this building. He would have been very much at home with the concrete work and workmen and would have enjoyed his site visits here.

It was a wonderful time to be a teenager in Canberra. We cycled to school each day from Narrabundah over the wooden bridge on Commonwealth Avenue. It seemed to rain more often in those days. When the Molonglo River flooded, the bridge got up a wobble and was closed, sometimes for days and we could not get to our school, then known as Canberra High School and now the ANU School of Art. At this end of the bridge we veered off left and up Marcus Clarke Street, past the Hotel Acton and

Beauchamp House. There were some interesting buildings here and in other parts of early Canberra. Maybe it was the quality of these places that first got me interested in architecture.

We played hide and seek in the house designed by Desbrowe Annear at the Forestry School in Yarralumla for Professor Max Jacobs, whose daughter Nancy was at school with us. That beautiful house in Banks Street (the only building by Annear in Canberra) is now under threat and is likely to be sold. As you know, any place owned by the government has heritage protection only as long as its purpose is funded by the government. If I may make any request of the Academy, Mr President, it is that you under no circumstances ever hand over the future of this building to a government, any government.

At the laying of the foundation stone here on 2 May 1958, Professor Oliphant said that the Academy had sought 'a fitting but modest headquarters' to symbolize the 'meaning of science and the spirit of the search for natural knowledge'. In this task, he said, they had been aided enormously by the architect ... 'with remarkable insight into our needs and with the boldness of the true contemporary artist, [Mr Grounds] has designed a building which we believe will prove to be one of the great creations of this period of architecture.'

Everybody who knows this place is proud of it. It was beautifully thought through at the beginning, was soundly put together and it was finely finished. It is in remarkable condition now because of the care and attention it has received through all of its life. The extraordinary generosity of its fellows and friends has kept it as modern as tomorrow and a unique symbol of the role of science in our society. It has an illustrious past and will have a great future.

Alan Roberts' story is a fine record of the first part of that life and I am pleased to launch this book into the world of today.

Bravely into a Man's World

The Canberra Times

December 2011

a review of
Marion Mahony Reconsidered
David Van Zanten

The first years of the twentieth century were in many countries rich indeed in art and design. In the busy field of architecture, the rigid rules of the past were cast aside for new building forms, with fresh and exciting combinations of functionalism and decoration. Within a few more years, some practitioners of the modern movement would strip their buildings of much of their delight and visual pleasure but, for the moment at least, architecture was about a new spirit of idealism and optimism. It was the age of finely rendered architectural drawings, heralding a big bold future for the world.

In Vienna, there were architects like Otto Wagner and Adolf Loos, celebrated recently in the splendid exhibition *Vienna: Art & Design* at the National Gallery of Victoria. In Chicago, it was the time of Daniel Burnham ('make no little plans') and of a young Frank Lloyd Wright, determined at all costs to be the first American architect of the new century. This new book is not about any of these iconic figures, but about a quiet young architect called Marion Lucy Mahony. She was for a few short years an assistant to Frank Lloyd Wright but for the rest of her life the staunchest disciple of Walter Burley Griffin, for whom she produced the wonderful set of architectural and landscape drawings that won the 1912 competition for the design of Australia's national capital city.

David Van Zanten has been researching Marion Mahony and her more famous husband in Chicago, Australia and India for more than forty years. Mahony, says Van Zanten, remains a subject of 'vivid interest' in the twin fields of architectural design and architectural representation, but he admits that her exact contribution is still 'frustratingly difficult to define'. In this latest search for the missing link, he has assembled four of the world's leading authorities on Mahony, each of whom casts a little more light on a complex character who lived and worked when international modern design was in its infancy.

The facts of Marion Mahony's life are well known. She was born in Chicago in 1871, the year of the fire that would lay waste to the city but bring about its re-birth. When she graduated in architecture from the Massachusetts Institute of Technology, she was only the second woman to do so. On her own account she designed a small and rather ordinary church and a handful of not very memorable houses before joining Frank Lloyd Wright in his Oak Park studio, where she developed her extraordinary skills as a delineator. Wright used Mahony's drawings as his own and published them widely. It is certain that without her 'ravishingly beautiful draftsmanship' Wright may not have risen so readily to the preeminence he firmly believed was his by birth.

Van Zanten says Mahony drew to attract attention, hardly a sin then or now in the world of architects and architecture. She laid out her drawings like the panels of Japanese prints and her trees were drawn in as much detail as the buildings, merging landscape and architecture into a single lyrical composition. While grateful for her drawings of his projects, Wright otherwise treated Mahony with indifference or worse. When Walter Burley Griffin came to work in Wright's studio, Mahony switched her allegiance to Griffin and then married him. Wright was predictably furious at losing his star illustrator to an upstart competitor, especially one who could win an international competition with drawings prepared by an ex-employee.

In 'Girl Talk', the first of the four long chapters in this book, Alice T Friedman writes that Mahony's parents introduced her to the world of musicians, poets, artists and religious reformers. Her belief in her own artistic gifts is expressed obliquely in her life's work *The Magic of America*, a monumental, rambling scrapbook which she described initially as a 'sort of account of Walt's work' but which went way beyond that into philosophy and politics and dreamland. She was 'eccentric, even annoying', says Friedman, but the products of her 'prodigious talents' made up for whatever trouble she caused.

In a second paper, 'Graphic Depictions', Paul Kruty notes that perspective drawings of buildings 'have their own conventions ... they have as much to do with image as with art or architecture'. In 1905, Wright was appointed as architect for the Unity Temple in Oak Park after the existing church was destroyed by fire. He turned to Mahony for a picture that would win over the congregation and she delivered the goods with a picture of a 'gleaming building' against a dark heathen background. The design clearly ignored the constraints of the budget as well as its surroundings, but both Wright and Mahony knew it is easier to get something built when you have a nice drawing of it.

The chapter 'Motifs and Motives' by long-time Griffin acolyte James Weirick concedes the sheer beauty and import of Mahony's work, but Weirick cautions against trying to fill all the gaps in her story. These gaps, he suggests, are the most intriguing aspect of her life. It is just not possible, he says, to make normal sense of Mahony's remarkable artistic abilities, nor of her worship of 'my Walt', while her 'strange omissions and silences' provoke 'enthusiasm and fascination' on the one hand and 'a slight sense of unease' on the other. Weirick stretches his metaphor past breaking point when he heaps praise on Mahony for her exquisite forest portraits, but then goes on to refer to the blank bits in her renderings as 'visual cues to the gaps and discontinuities' of her life.

Mahony always denied any role in the design of Canberra, saying only that 'my work on the plans for the Federal Capital attracted a little notice'. There is no doubt however in Weirick's mind that the 'great achievements' of the Griffins in Melbourne—Newman College, the Café Australia and the Capitol Theatre—all benefited from Mahony's extraordinary artistic talents. The Capitol Theatre in particular, described by Robin Boyd as 'the best cinema that was ever built or is ever likely to be built', has a decorated interior that Weirick says is unquestionably a product of Marion's creative imagination.

In a final paper, Anna Rubbo confirms the opinion of Weirick and others that Marion Mahony chose to work at the margins during her lifetime and has been accordingly marginalised ever since. She started her career, says Rubbo, as an 'outspoken but secondary voice in Frank Lloyd Wright's office' and ended it as a 'largely unrecognised public commentator from the sidelines'. Her low public profile in Australia with Walter was quiet by choice. But after Walter's death in India, she became obsessed with the ideas of Rudolph Steiner and anthroposophy, which permeates *The Magic of America* like a 'vengeful angel'. Her magnum opus became unpublishable, a madness that set all against her when she went home to Chicago and which has isolated her ever since in the story of twentieth century architecture.

With all her faults and imperfections, the uniqueness of Marion Mahony's achievements should never be underestimated. She walked bravely into a man's world where she not only survived but flourished. Her magnificent renderings for the design of Canberra can be seen at a fraction of their true size (and impact) in a number of books on Griffin's work. Her originals, truly some of Australia's national treasures, are held safe by our National Archives and are put on show from time to time. Canberra's centenary year of 2013 is bound to be one of these times. If you have not ever seen them, or even if you have, behold with awe the sheer power of the finest architectural renderings by a truly remarkable architect.

The City and the Lake

The Canberra Times
May 2013

Coloured drawings, models and digital fly-throughs have been issued showing how Canberra's Civic Centre could be linked to Lake Burley Griffin. We are told this is a 'transformational project' integral to 'realising the potential of the city'. Sites have been identified and reserved for a convention centre, a 30,000 seat rectangular stadium and a regional aquatic centre. There will be apartment buildings for up to 20,000 new city edge residents and strategically placed multi-use car parks for events and commuters.

It all sounds wonderful, but unless these things are in the right place and joined properly to each other and to the existing areas around City Hill I fear this will be a transformation we will live to regret.

They say that God is in the details, but it helps a lot if the basic idea is good. Ten years ago, The Griffin Legacy looked at some of the unrealised ideas in the Griffin designs for Canberra to see what could sensibly be added to what has been built so far. A subsequent Amendment 60 to the National Capital Plan sought to turn the forgotten Constitution Avenue into Griffin's municipal high street, a modern day mixed-use boulevard with broad sidewalks and sunny outdoor dining. Sadly, good intentions and happy pedestrians were lost under the iron fist of the traffic engineers, and we have heard nothing about Constitution Avenue for a year or more.

Another Legacy Amendment showed how the city centre might be connected to the West Basin of the lake. Amendment 61 called for 'legible networks of paths and streets that extend the city to the lake'. It also foresaw a lakeside site on Griffin's water axis for a significant public building or landscape area. Buildings would be generally low rise and there would be a continuous promenade on the north shore of the lake from Commonwealth Park to behind the National Museum. Amendment 61 has spawned the 'City to the Lake' project, but in the process it has introduced ideas that will work against the stated aims to link the city to the waterfront. Sadly, the chance to be a little bit special has also been lost.

The scale of the City to the Lake project, the layout of roads and the allocation of building sites seem quite unresolved and a number of largish public buildings sit uncomfortably on unsuitable sites. Amendment 61 requires a 55 metre wide waterfront promenade made up of a pedestrian walk, a recreation and park zone, a cycleway and a two-lane street. Instead we have the narrowest of footpaths plus a timber boardwalk of unspecified width hovering over the water, interrupted by a narrow sandy beach and covered full-size swimming pools.

This 'aquatic facility' is supposed to compensate for the loss of the existing Olympic pool but it is all rather remote from city workers. As for the artificial beach, Brisbane's South Bank is a pleasant enough suburban park in a rather more benign climate, but its swimming hole and fun park image are, I suggest, not good models for the central areas of Canberra. The Civic pools must in due course be replaced but they need not move far. A modern and accessible swimming centre would fit very nicely in the top corner of Commonwealth Park right across Parkes Way from the existing pool.

A new convention and exhibition centre, a building crying out for a proud waterfront site, has been tucked away in a corner of London Circuit with a view of nothing. It should be given a plum site on the western shore, ideally on Griffin's water axis and with a watergate and ferry terminal worthy of the national capital city. A huge football stadium has been squeezed on to the site of the Civic pool. This is surely the last thing you would want along Constitution Avenue, a major city street and a vital pedestrian zone day and night. If we really must have a stadium in the city, it would be better to look at sites like Northbourne Oval, which is close to the main transport routes into and out of the city and within walking distance of hotels and thousands of houses and flats.

Town and city centres which are pleasant for residents and visitors alike most often have a 'fine grain' and an attractive human scale, with streets of various widths and lengths and lanes and pocket parks for slow or faster movement along a range of routes and addresses. This fine grain allows for visual variety in building types and uses and supports human comfort and a sense of safety and control.

Manuka, for example, has a fine grain with generous footpaths and many possible options to move about or sit and relax. The structure of Civic is at a coarser grain, but it is still possible to move comfortably across and through it, particularly in older parts where there are service lanes behind the shops and offices. Amendment 61 suggests such opportunities, but the proposed pattern does not set out to make a lunchtime stroll from the city to the lake a memorable experience.

Streets should take you places you want to go at speeds you choose to travel. Kingston Foreshore has shown us how not to do this, with the boat harbour now walled off from every part of Kingston and no promise that the journey is worth taking. The same merciless superblock geometry has been applied in the West Basin proposal, when a less formal street pattern and smaller building blocks could help develop a unique character for the place. 'I live at Acton' could be an adequate description of a desirable lifestyle, not just a postcode.

As with most waterfront cities, the roads that matter are the roads down to the water for these are the lifeblood of the place. Streets and walkways to and from West Basin should link effortlessly with similar routes into the city centre and on to the inner north.

Our city planners have only ever seen Northbourne Avenue as a highway into town, not as the great boulevard it could be. Tree-lined streets like Lonsdale Street and Torrens Street play valuable supporting roles but more such connections could be threaded through and across the city centre to enrich the city fabric. For West Basin and everywhere else in town, it is the narrow streets and laneways that should be laid out first. It will take guts to defy the traffic engineers, but if we don't we might as well live in Los Angeles or Dubai.

The Griffin legacy

Bowen Place Crossing

Architecture Australia

April 2016

The scale of Walter Burley Griffin's design for Canberra is quite beyond the visual comprehension of any ground level observer. Nevertheless, his marvellous landscape composition has served the city and the nation well for more than a hundred years and has demonstrated the worth of Daniel Burnham's plea to 'make no little plans'. With Griffin's main lines firmly established on the ground, the attention of the federal government and the National Capital Authority has moved in recent times to the creation of a finer grain for the Central National Area and a careful filling in of the bits that people should be able to use. Once described by Griffin as an 'accessible but still quiet area', the southern lakeshore of the central basin is one such precinct which is developing as a very successful linear park.

The new Bowen Place Crossing fits into a small corner of this 'still quiet area' at the southern end of Kings Avenue Bridge. It is the most recent addition to a collection of thoughtful landscape insertions bringing human scale and varied character to Canberra's formal public spaces and the National Capital Authority is to be congratulated for the high standard of its design and execution. A principal objective for this project was to ensure the safe and separated movement of cars, pedestrians and cyclists at road level and at lake level, but the Authority was looking for more than just clever traffic engineering. With a lengthy process of option studies, public consultations and finally an invited competition among five highly qualified design teams, the Authority was after a design that would address the national agenda and the wider community and at the same time integrate with the existing landscape and built context in a 'robust, sensitive and enduring manner'.

The winning design by LahzNimmo with Spackman Mossop Michaels is refreshingly minimalist in form and detail. The competition jury, chaired by ACT Government Architect Alastair Swayn, found the design 'elegant, logical and direct'. An early reviewer of the competition entries, misunderstanding the aims of the competition and more at ease perhaps with established urban squares in older cities than with the clear light and soft edges of Canberra, lamented that the winning design did not do 'anything remarkable' to transform the space into a place. Now that it is open for business, the project can be seen to do all it was asked to do with a generosity that will moreover allow it to develop further over time.

Asked in 1957 for his view as to whether federal expenditure could turn the largely empty Canberra into a capital city worthy of the nation, the British architect and town planner Sir William Holford suggested that high quality urban infrastructure in Canberra would always be a very good investment. Bowen Place Crossing is such a good investment. It sits comfortably at the starting point of a promenade of national significance and resolves modern day problems of movement and safety with confidence and considerable panache.

The challenge to separate motorists from cyclists and pedestrians brought a number of interesting ideas from the other teams invited to participate in the design competition. One proposal offered short cuts at a steeper grade for those in a hurry, hinting at some local knowledge of Canberra's peak hour conflicts between lycra clad cyclists and slower moving walkers and joggers and baby strollers.

There were also some dramatic 'landscape rooms' and a colourful 'underpass room' plus a suggestion to float the full length of the roadway above the ground level. Presenting as straightforward geometry, architectural elegance and clean detailing, the LahzNimmo design avoids tricky turns, junctions and abrupt level changes and focuses instead on a wide sweeping ramp which straightens out at the bottom and flows under an almost invisible roadway.

The design anticipates the possible expansion of the adjacent Australian National Gallery with hopes for 'meaningful connection' to Harry Howard's wonderful sculpture garden and the marsh pond. The Crossing is however a functional landscape construction rather than a place of assembly or reflection and accordingly picks up on the quality engineering style of the busy traffic interchange by Johnson Pilton Walker at the north end of the bridge. Pedestrian underpasses are often shunned as unsafe and the design therefore ensures long clear sightlines with no opportunities for concealment. Vandal proof light fixtures high on the Corten inner wall and in the soffit of the pedestrian underpass address concerns for nighttime safety. A subtle swelling of the pathway at the centre of the underpass makes that part of the journey seem less daunting, a reminder that the entasis of Greek columns recognises that the eye can play tricks with straight lines and on occasion needs a helping hand to make things feel right.

The durable and visually interesting palette of precast concrete, washed aggregate paving and granite setts is almost a lingua franca for public places in Canberra and elsewhere. Junctions are neatly made and steel balustrades and handrails are remarkably smooth to the touch. Lines on the ground to separate users are thankfully absent but small stencilled signs remind us this is a shared pathway and advise one to move slowly, keep left and give way. The soft landscape has a few scattered trees in a gently sloping green sward with a planted 'rain garden' to collect and filter stormwater before it enters the lake.

An attractive and photogenic spot, the intermittent arrival of people of wildly differing age and appearance and modes of transport moving one way or the other makes for a fascinating vicarious experience. Perhaps in time there will be a sculpture or two swaying in the wind. A place of movement rather than rest, the peaceful setting might nevertheless benefit from the presence of a few wooden benches off to the side of the ramp where people could take a well earned break and enjoy the passing parade.

The significance of the word 'crossing' in the name of this place will not be lost on those who came to Canberra before there was a lake. For Canberra's first fifty years as Australia's seat of government, and prior to that when the Canberra valley was a gentle collection of farms and sheep stations, the Molonglo River flooded regularly. Griffin's designs showed a causeway but this was never built and residents and visitors had to rely on a temporary

Brett Boardman

wooden bridge and two low level river crossings. The most popular of these routes linking north and south Canberra, and the first to be closed when there were heavy rains, was known as Scott's Crossing, which started halfway along Kings Avenue almost exactly at the new Bowen Place Crossing. The road crossed the river near what is now Aspen Island and ran in a long straight line to Blundell's Cottage and St John's Church and on to the Civic Centre. In the LahzNimmo diagram, diagonal view lines at road level and at lake level tie the new crossing lightly but clearly to the Carillon on Aspen Island, a reminder of earlier times in a town where it is easy for many of today's leaders and developers to believe that history started last week.

Faculty of Education University of Sydney

I had no abiding philosophy to develop or test but there was this immense opportunity as an architect of the right age at a time when Canberra was going through an amazing change

Roger Pegrum | **A Canberra Architect**

www.ingramcontent.com/pod-product-compliance
Lightning Source LLC
Chambersburg PA
CBHW060803150426
42813CB00059B/2880